An introduction
to systems analysis
techniques

An introduction to systems analysis techniques

MARK LEJK AND DAVID DEEKS

UNIVERSITY OF SUNDERLAND

PRENTICE HALL

LONDON   NEW YORK   TORONTO   SYDNEY   TOKYO   SINGAPORE
MADRID   MEXICO CITY   MUNICH   PARIS

First published 1998 by
Prentice Hall
A Pearson Education company
Edinburgh Gate, Harlow
Essex CM20 2JE England

Typeset in 9.75/13pt Sabon

Printed and bound in Great Britain by
Redwood Books, Trowbridge, Wiltshire

Library of Congress Cataloging-in-Publication Data

Available from the publisher

British Library Cataloguing in Publication Data

A catalogue record for this book is available from
the British Library

3   4   5   02   01   00   99

Contents

Foreword

This book will introduce you to the skills and understanding needed to deliver technically proficient solutions into an enthused and accepting human community. The authors are very experienced in meeting these twin challenges – present in all successfully implemented systems – and have enthusiastically sent thousands of undergraduates down the road to success.

The business of putting together a successful computer-based information system is slowly becoming better understood as more experience of the nature of the challenge is gained. Only a few decades have elapsed during the life of these sorts of system, so we are still learning and still adjusting our approach. However, some important principles have already emerged. We have learnt to differentiate between those in which *software engineers* produce *software products* and those environments where *system developers* implement *information systems*. The former case is concerned with product specifications and the management of software 'factories'. The latter is concerned with the preparation and embedding of an information system into an organizational context.

When a system developer walks away from the successful implementation of a good system, what has been achieved is the acceptance and efficient operation of a technical computer system by a human community. The system has both a technical and a social dimension – it is a *socio-technical* system. The project plan will have allowed for the evolution of the technical aspects of the system with the active involvement of the human community that will operate it.

If these are the characteristics of a successfully implemented system, it is obvious that those charged with the development task should understand and be skilled at both social and technical aspects of systems. Just about the worst kind of description of this process is conveyed by referring to the project analyst as an *engineer* because this conveys the concept of an all-seeing, all-knowing being devising solutions which are lowered into position and switched on. Such an approach is highly inappropriate to cope with the social aspects of information systems. A more fitting metaphor is implied by the word *developer* because the indication is that of joint discovery and refinement by the users and the systems analyst of particular system components which are effective in achieving project objectives.

The systems analyst as *developer* underpins the theme of this book.

Enjoy your study.

R. T. Bell BSc PGCE
Director
School of Computing and Information Systems
University of Sunderland
February 1997

Acknowledgements

We would like to acknowledge the help of the following people in this project.

- Colleague and Senior Lecturer Sue Stirk, who carefully checked through our early attempts and gave useful advice.
- Jackie Harbor of Prentice Hall who accepted our initial proposal and then sought out critical reviews on early versions of the text, thus passing on valuable input from a wide range of experts.
- Students on the following University of Sunderland course modules, for whom the final draft was piloted as core text and who provided many useful comments.
    BTEC HND Computing, Systems Analysis and Design
    BA Business Computing, Systems Analysis and Design
    BA Accounting and Computing, Systems Analysis and Design
    BA Business and Finance, Business Systems Analysis
    Post-Graduate Certificate in Health Information Systems, Systems Analysis and Design
- Mark Deeks, who enthusiastically offered rigorous criticism in the even-handed way which only an *A-level Computing* son can muster, and Lynda Deeks for her diligent proof-reading.
- Maureen, Emma, Katie and Matthew Lejk for their support and encouragement.

All comments were noted carefully, and most resulted in enhancements. Our own input, based upon the materials and methods which we use in class, has thus been supplemented by other teachers, systems analysts and students. In this way we have done our best to ensure that the following text is both academically sound, and easily understood. We would like to thank all who contributed to the project.

Mark Lejk BA BSc MBCS CEng
David Deeks MSc CertEd FIAP
School of Computing and Information Systems
University of Sunderland
February 1997

Introduction

If you have picked up this book you must have at least a passing interest in systems analysis. Perhaps you are completely new to the subject, or perhaps you know a little already but need to learn more. Whatever your reason, we hope that you will read on and discover that our aim has been to make it as accessible as possible.

We have concentrated upon only a selection of techniques – most being those which are in widest use within business application development environments and commonly found in HND and degree computing courses, as well as an increasing number of post-graduate 'conversion' ones. We introduce these techniques in ways which have been found to work best with the students that we teach. This is not to suggest that there are no difficult bits, but simply that we would be hard pressed to think of ways to make them easier.

- For continuity purposes a student assessment system is revisited several times as different techniques are explored, but we have included other scenarios when we feel they do a better job.

- Whenever possible we describe the application of each technique in a series of clearly defined steps.

- We include hardly any self-study exercises. This may seem a little surprising, but there are two reasons: first we have assumed that, as in our own school, students will be given tutor-designed ones appropriate to the course being taught; secondly, in our experience students never use book-based exercises as they are intended – being more likely to read the question and immediately look up the answer. We therefore concentrate on giving clearly worked examples within the main text, describing problems and then showing step by step how to solve them.

- Each chapter ends with a short paragraph summarizing what has been covered, and lists any recommended further reading on the subject. All such texts are personal favourites, and have been chosen for their accessible reading style as well as their academic correctness.

We spend quite a lot of time on data flow diagrams (DFDs). The reason is that this book is angled towards the *business* end of systems analysis – the *human* end – and DFDs are an extremely useful interface between user and computing practitioner. You will then find that, whilst we cover some aspects of design, there is a lot more about analysis. This is because even the most creative systems designer would find it difficult to communicate his grand schemes without a firm foundation in analysis techniques; a bit like expecting an artist to paint a picture, having been taught how to visualise a scene but with inadequate instruction in how to mix colours or create different brush strokes.

So, systems analysis is all about techniques, right? Techniques which allow the analyst to turn situations into diagrams, mess around with them a bit and turn them into systems? Well, partly right. But the fact is that you could become the best user of systems analysis techniques that the world has ever seen, and still not be a useful systems analyst. Academically above criticism, but in practical terms of little use.

The reason is simple. There are few opportunities these days for practitioners in any profession to work in isolation. For the systems analyst there are two major areas of constraint. Firstly, there are decisions to be made as to which analysis approach best suits the circumstance in which the work is to be carried out. The first chapter is designed to help with this by giving a brief background as to the alternatives available. Secondly, it is usually necessary to work as a member of a team of people, bringing with it responsibilities of communication, co-operation, collaboration and negotiation not only with other team members, but also with the world at large – the *users*. The last chapter, therefore, has something to say about the environment in which the analyst is expected to work, and gives some help with regard to establishing objectives and managing a project.

This book is like a sandwich. In between the two chapters referred to above you will find the 'filling' – a practical introduction to widely used systems analysis techniques. It is only by becoming proficient in the tools of your trade that you will be able to make a technical contribution to your systems analysis team: making choices, influencing decisions, communicating with people, applying techniques and working as an effective team member.

Welcome to the world of systems analysis.

Systems analysis within the overall systems development process

1.1 Setting the scene

1.1.1 Introduction

The main part of this book is primarily concerned with helping you get to grips with systems analysis techniques. If this is literally *all* you want to do, then you may like to skip to the next chapter. If you are new to the whole concept of computer systems development however, and/or would appreciate some explanation as to where systems analysis is found within the development process – read on. The background which follows is by no means exhaustive, but is intended to give an initial feel for where systems analysis 'sits'.

1.1.2 Structured analysis

To begin with, we need to get one fundamental point clear. Simply by using the term *systems analysis*, or referring to the role of *systems analyst*, to the computer systems development world at large we have already laid some implied cards on the table. We have effectively announced that we are talking about an approach to computer systems development that is known as a *structured analysis* one. There are others, and this chapter includes a brief introduction to one or two. The fact is, however, that on those occasions where a formal method is utilized (and much development still takes place without one), the majority of business application computer systems are currently developed using a strategy which embodies structured analysis techniques.

1.1.3 Techniques, methods, strategies

Students who are new to computer systems development often become confused by the difference between *techniques*, *methods* and *strategies*. We have already used all three terms. Some clarification is in order – see Figure 1.1.

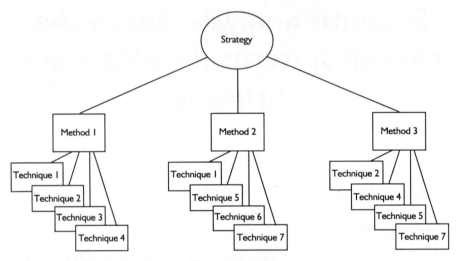

Figure 1.1   A systems development hierarchy

Techniques are at the lowest level. These are designed to do a particular job within the systems analysis process. Much of this book describes techniques – data flow diagrams, logical data structures, etc. A systems analysis *method* (or sometimes the more grandiose term *methodology* is used) will embody a number of techniques, each chosen for its appropriateness to a particular task within the overall aim of the method. The Structured Systems Analysis and Design Method (SSADM) is one of the best known published structured analysis and design methods, and Jackson Structured Programming (JSP) is similarly widely known as an approach to structured programming. There are many others, as well as even more unpublished ones, commonly derived through custom and practice within individual organizations.

A computer systems development *strategy* will commonly be agreed within a particular organization and may involve the use of, for instance, SSADM for certain parts of the development process or for certain types of system but may use other methods for other situations. The same strategy could include the use of JSP for

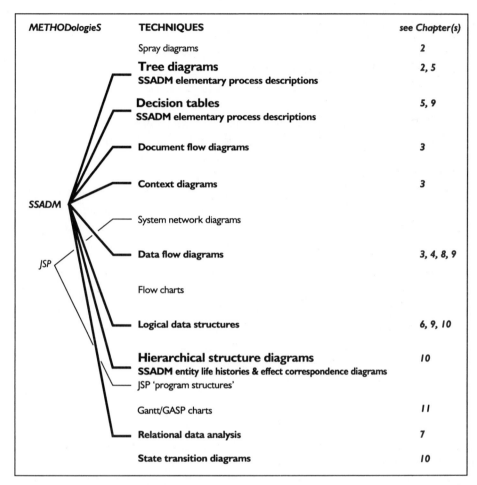

METHODologieS	TECHNIQUES	see Chapter(s)
	Spray diagrams	2
	Tree diagrams	2, 5
	SSADM elementary process descriptions	
	Decision tables	5, 9
	SSADM elementary process descriptions	
	Document flow diagrams	3
	Context diagrams	3
SSADM	System network diagrams	
	Data flow diagrams	3, 4, 8, 9
JSP	Flow charts	
	Logical data structures	6, 9, 10
	Hierarchical structure diagrams	10
	SSADM entity life histories & effect correspondence diagrams	
	JSP 'program structures'	
	Gantt/GASP charts	11
	Relational data analysis	7
	State transition diagrams	10

Figure 1.2   The relationship between methods and techniques

designing the structures of large 'data handling' types of program but an alternative for other circumstances.

Just to give you the idea, Figure 1.2 shows a selection of techniques and relates appropriate ones to SSADM and JSP. As this book is about systems analysis, the SSADM ones are highlighted. There are many more techniques than those shown – including others used by SSADM – but we have made sure that all of the techniques described in this book are included.

There is no need for you to worry about the detail at this stage – simply accept that there are many techniques, many methods which incorporate a variety of them, and that organisations can decide upon a wide range of systems development strategies.

1.1.4 Communication is the key

If you are an aspiring systems analyst, it is easy to become intimidated by all the things which need to be considered in order to see a system's development through to a satisfactory conclusion. The basic requirements of successful systems analysis are, however, an ability to think analytically, and communicate effectively with the prospective user – and the programmer, unless you are covering this role yourself (as an 'analyst–programmer'). It is the user's job to consider carefully what is being offered, highlight any perceived shortcomings and provide alternative suggestions from a user viewpoint. The programmer must ensure understanding of what is being specified/discussed, and communicate clearly any queries or alternative suggestions from a software development perspective. The user and programmer are not therefore free from a need to communicate, but it is the responsibility of the analyst to be the 'bridge' between them, ensuring that all communication is clear and acted upon.

The most common reason for new systems to fail is poor communication somewhere along the line. Use of well-proven analysis techniques is a major factor in improving communication and thus ensuring mutual understanding at each stage of a system's development. By mastering the techniques found within this book, you will have the requisite tools at your disposal. The development structure in which you utilize them will then be up to you, and the rest of this chapter is intended to give an initial glimpse of the framework within which you will make such decisions.

1.1.5 Planning, control, progress

There are many ways of approaching the development of a computer system, some more appropriate to certain situations than others. Whatever the circumstance, the important word to note is *development* – for this implies planning, control and progress. This means that the development should take place as quickly and efficiently as the situation allows. Undue adherence to long-winded approaches using large project teams has just as often led to failure, as has the 'hacker' out for a quick and easy solution. With the first, costs can escalate whilst an actual working solution remains out of reach. The second often leads to dissatisfied users who are left to find the design and programming faults in a system which has been passed off as complete and which turns out at best to be a partially working *prototype*. This has led to prototyping itself gaining something of a bad reputation, whilst the rapid development possible with the latest application software can increasingly allow legitimate and cost-effective use of the approach – as long as it remains within a structured development framework. The largest proportion of business application computer systems is currently developed using a strategy which embodies structured analysis supported by prototyping. More about both of these later.

Many approaches have therefore been devised, but they are not self-exclusive. Even the development of a system using the full, traditional, Systems Development Life Cycle (SDLC – more on this below) is now usually undertaken with the incorporation of one or more of the later introductions. The analyst will commonly play a key role in the decision as to which approach to use. Any such decision should be based upon an assessment as to how best to gain the *fastest progress* through the necessary level of *planning and control*.

It is time to give some background to help you make such decisions.

1.2 The Systems Development Life Cycle (SDLC)

1.2.1 What it is

The SDLC grew up in the late 1960s/early 1970s and was really the first successful attempt at a fully documented approach. It is now viewed as traditional (or old-hat, depending upon your age), but it is certainly comprehensive. It is also extremely logical – ensuring that all stages of the development of a system are thought about, planned, monitored and completed. Whilst it grew up in the era of large mainframe computer systems, it can still provide a valuable checklist of things to consider, no matter what the environment. It thus has much to teach us, and for this reason its stages are listed in Section 1.2.2. For the analysis and design stages of large projects, the Structured Systems Analysis and Design Method (SSADM) can for instance be readily mapped onto the SDLC, and would not have become so popular if it were not so. SSADM has been adopted for all areas of business computer systems development within British government control, and many other organizations use greater or lesser parts of it.

1.2.2 The stages of the SDLC

Whilst the SDLC can be separated into anything between five and nine stages, the most common are probably the six shown in Figure 1.3. The indication as to which techniques are appropriate to the stages is by no means exhaustive but is intended simply to give a feel for typical uses of some of the structured analysis techniques which you will find in this book.

The diagram should be read in context, for it has already been made clear that the systems analyst is much more than simply an expert in the use of techniques. He or she is involved at every stage of the development process, acting as

		(Typical systems analysis techniques found in this book)
STAGE 1	**Preliminary investigation** *Gain clear understanding of current system,* *Summarise findings to management - including* *whether to proceed with next stage.*	context diagram data flow diagram data modelling normalization
STAGE 2	**Systems analysis** *Define business requirements (software) for new* *system (hardware requirements finalized during* *and after design phase), prepare system* *requirements report, evaluate alternatives,* *prepare Request For Proposal (RFP).*	context diagram data flow diagram data modelling normalization
STAGE 3	**System design** *Define technical design, establish controls, prepare* *design documentation, use CASE tools/prototyping,* *build project dictionary.*	data flow diagram data modelling normalization entity life history state transition diagram
STAGE 4	**System construction** *Create or select software required by new system,* *design, choose supplier, train users and operators, test system.*	
STAGE 5	**Systems implementation** *Get new system running, create final operating* *documentation and procedures, begin to use system.*	
STAGE 6	**Evaluation** *Check new system meets objectives, make adjustments.*	

Figure 1.3   The traditional Systems Development Life Cycle

user–programmer liaison, getting involved with training and user documentation, testing, evaluation, etc. Note also that the SDLC is a *cycle* – the review which occurs at the end can easily result in 'fine tuning' or the decision to add extra facilities, which can then begin the whole process again.

1.2.3 The appropriateness of the SDLC

The full SDLC remains most appropriate to situations where there are predictable information systems requirements. This would include circumstances where users have a clear idea of their needs, or where there is an existing system with a clearly defined structure. Such a situation will be found in systems involving the entry of data from input documents with high transaction and processing volumes, requiring validation of data input and encompassing several departments. The complexity will often necessitate a long development timetable, and development by project teams.

The SDLC approach is highly project manageable as the stages can be clearly identified, scheduled, monitored and controlled. Sometimes the creation of the project plan is seen as a separate step following stage 1, but this implies that stage 1 itself is not planned, and in any instance project planning and control is really an on-going task, implicit within the whole systems development process. We return to such aspects in the closing chapter – by which time you will have become familiar with a range of analysis techniques.

1.3 The structured analysis approach

The techniques found in the rest of this book are based upon this approach. Conceived in the mid-to-late 1970s, structured analysis focuses upon what a system does rather than how it does it. This means that the emphasis is logical rather than physical, addressing what the system is meant to accomplish. Looking at it another way, the structured analysis approach is based on the assumption that the procedures used within organizations are stable, with the data stored and used in a way that simply supports the procedures.

The main characteristic of structured analysis is the *top down functional decomposition* of the system. The conversion from the physical to the logical view is handled early in the development process. The traditional approach has been that the physical view begins with document flow diagrams being prepared. In practice, it does not really matter whether it begins with documents (leading to data flows), or by talking to people (thereby identifying processes) – but one way or another data flow diagrams are constructed which show the physical system (explained in Chapters 3 and 4) and allow progression to a view of what is logically *happening* (such logicalization is demonstrated in Chapter 8). Logical data structures (covered in Chapters 6 and 7) are used to show entities and their relationships, i.e. what is logically *there*.

With structured analysis, stage 1 of the SDLC will usually involve the decomposition of the higher levels of the system – further decomposition taking place in stages 2 and 3, and even as far as stage 4. As you become familiar with the techniques described in this book, you will better appreciate how they fit in with the SDLC as shown in the illustration.

SSADM builds upon the structured analysis approach by providing three fundamental views of a system, i.e. process-centred, data-centred and event-centred. It is designed to produce documentation at every stage that will be understandable by a third party. Taken to the extreme this can allow a variety of suppliers to combine in the development of a system, without necessarily even needing to know each other's identity. This feature makes it attractive where high security is an important factor – for instance in banking, or applications for the armed forces.

1.4 Prototyping

1.4.1 What it is

Prototyping is not a formal approach as such, but we are going to spend a little time covering it for reasons which will become evident. Traditionally, those who have supported prototyping have often been seen as 'hackers' who have little understanding of 'proper' methods and who may produce a result quickly, but with little chance of its being any good in the long run. Prototyping is now gaining recognition, however, as a technique which has its place within an overall strategy, for it can provide an important complement to the documentation created by a structured analysis approach. SSADM version 4.2 formally acknowledges the part that prototyping can play, saying that it should be used as part of the Requirements Specification stage *in order to describe relevant parts in an animated form, for the user's benefit.*

It has some undoubted strengths. It allows the demonstration of the system at various stages of the development process – involving users to ensure that the development is satisfactory before progressing to the next stage, and providing a useful platform to establish their requirements before having them check the next update. It is therefore part of an iterative, or evolutionary, approach.

1.4.2 Within the SDLC

The traditional SDLC approach and the increasing use of prototyping may initially seem to be mutually exclusive. Look back at the SDLC stage 3 (Section 1.2.2), however. Even within the SDLC as it was developed more than 25 years ago, prototyping was seen to have its place – albeit often a minor one. It is now so much easier to create a prototype than it was then, particularly with increasingly sophisticated Computer Aided Software Engineering (CASE) tools, that the benefits are increasingly appreciated and acted upon. As the analyst utilises appropriate techniques to document the proposed system in order to gain user acceptance, he or she can reinforce and clarify the intended design by demonstrating a prototype.

1.4.3 Strengths

Prototyping's obvious strengths lie within areas of unique application settings, or where developers have little or no experience (probably more than any other, this use has given prototyping its bad name among system professionals), or where costs or risks of error may be high. It can be an extremely efficient means of establishing user requirements, by gaining their feedback stage by stage as the system evolves.

Prototyping has an important role to play where future users have no computing experience, and has been shown to have a strong demystifying effect. Users who are involved in the systems development process are invariably more accommodating when the time comes to go live – and this can be an important commercial consideration, particularly for the small software company developing a system for an important client. There is another important commercial advantage for the small software house: prototyping can be used as a powerful persuader along with the systems tender, by being able to *demonstrate* what can be done.

Because of the inherent need to produce a result quickly, prototyping has really only come into its own along with the availability of high level programming languages. It is undoubtedly a rising star within systems development strategies and, along with the continued rapid evolution of user friendly development software, is quickly becoming a major one.

1.4.4 How to apply it

When using the prototyping approach it is important to firstly consider how it can best be applied. It is possible for instance to provide users with menu structures prior to developing actual facilities, or to develop one facility completely before going on to develop others – or both.

It is worth noting again a point stressed in Section 1.3 – i.e. the need to make your intentions *understandable to a third party*, the potential user of the system. The creation of an initial prototype can do much to demonstrate exactly what it is you are proposing to develop – so what should it consist of?

On the one hand, the initial prototype can incorporate a complete menu structure which does not actually do anything. This gives the prospective user a good idea of the *look and feel* of the proposed system, as well as demonstrating that you have thought of all the *facilities* that will be needed. Alternatively, one key facility can be selected and developed completely. This is good for demonstrating the likely *functionality* of the system. Ideally, it is best for the analyst to aim for *both* of these – attempting to develop much of the final menu structure, but ensuring that at least one facility works completely.

As already explained, prototyping used to the full employs an iterative approach: i.e. with regular reference to the user. The prototype thus steadily develops into a completed system with which the user is familiar, and for which he or she feels ownership.

1.5 Other approaches

1.5.1 Data centred

This approach is another which originated in the seventies. It is based on the premise that the basic *data* that an organization uses is stable, whereas the *procedures* are not. It often comes under the umbrella term *Information Engineering*.

In this approach, data becomes a separate resource within an organization and processes become merely a means of transforming it. The design of the database becomes the most important aspect.

The data-centred approach usually incurs a heavy front end loading in terms of cost and time before results are produced. Once the front end investment has been made, however, it is said that systems can be developed more rapidly than with the structured approach.

The data-centred approach tends to have a centralist, 'big computer' orientation, and is usually dependent upon one systems consultancy/development team seeing the whole process through to the end.

1.5.2 Object oriented

This is one of the more recent developments. To someone new to the world of computer systems, it is perhaps one of the most difficult concepts to describe. In a sense it combines the structured analysis 'what a system does' view and the data-centred 'what information the system uses' view. It results in a number of standard *modules* within a system which have predetermined effects upon the data that is sent their way, and which are called upon by any part of the system that requires that effect to take place.

One way of appreciating an object-oriented view of things, is to wait until Chapters 3 and 4 have introduced you to data flow diagrams – for these provide a convenient way of illustrating the concept. Instead of looking upon processes, data flows and data stores as being discrete 'things', the object-oriented view would look for combinations of processing which could be viewed as being the same – and each would become an identifiable *object* available to all parts of the system. Thus, a data flow diagram illustrating one part of the system could to all intents and purposes contain a sub-process which carried out the same basic function as a sub-process in another part of the system. These would become one *object*.

In theory, the object-oriented approach creates systems which are easily catalogued and managed. To date we have discovered very few examples of fully working systems and thus cannot yet take a firm view.

1.5.3 Soft systems

Structured analysis approaches are often called 'hard' – not in the sense of difficult but more in the sense of concrete. It is assumed that the system has a goal, that the problems are easily identifiable and the requirements are largely known. All you need is some tried and tested techniques to set the ball rolling. But what if the problems are not clear? What if there are several different points of view? What if there is a general sense that things need improving but no one knows how or exactly what? This is where the Soft Systems approach comes in strongly. It was developed by Peter Checkland from Lancaster University and is a very sophisticated participative analysis of the problem situation.

Using cartoon-like diagrams called *Rich Pictures*, the participants build up a picture of the organization under study and represent communicaton flows, processes, areas of conflict, external observers and interactions. The aim of this is to help in the construction of a root definition which expresses very concisely what the system is. The method goes on to build conceptual models which would support the requirements outlined in the root definition. By comparing these models with the original expression of the problem, it is possible to formulate some desirable changes and actions to improve the problem situation.

In the most recent versions of SSADM, Soft Systems has been proposed as a possible 'front-end' to structured analysis approaches as it helps very much in formulating the problem.

1.6 A vital role

We are all familiar with press reports of major systems that have failed to achieve the desired outcome. For every major one that gets reported, there are dozens of smaller ones that never gain such public notoriety. But what is meant by 'failed to achieve the desired outcome'? Usually it means that the prospective *user* has judged the system to be to a greater or lesser extent *unusable*. This is the rationale behind the assertion that, when deciding upon a strategy for systems development, the systems analyst should first consider how best to involve the user at every stage. Prototyping provides an increasingly effective opportunity to do so.

The systems analyst has a vital role to play at all times within a system's development, beginning with the initial decision as to which development strategy to utilize. The key consideration is how best to gain the fastest progress through the necessary level of planning and control. Use of well-proven analysis techniques is a major factor in improving communication and thus ensuring mutual understanding between developers and users at each stage of a system's development.

The traditional SDLC still has much to offer in terms of an overall framework – but this does not imply that the full-blown SDLC is necessarily applicable to most projects. The structured analysis techniques which form the main part of this book can of course be used in isolation, but any project needs control of some kind if it is to succeed. The SDLC provides a convenient linear checklist of tasks to be undertaken or ignored as appropriate.

Summary

This chapter began by introducing the concepts of techniques, methods and strategies within computer systems development. It introduced you to the systems development life cycle, structured analysis, prototyping, and data-centred, and soft systems object-oriented approaches. It ended by stressing the importance of the role of the systems analyst within the systems development process. The purpose has been to give you an idea as to where systems analysis fits in the overall scheme of things. It can provide you with an absorbing and fulfilling career. First, however, you need to learn the tools of the trade – the techniques which allow the analyst to analyse, communicate, influence and gain consensus.

Read on!

Further reading

J. Tudor I. J. Tudor, *Systems Analysis and Design – a Comparison of Structured Methods*, Blackwell, Oxford, 1995.
P. Checkland, *Systems Thinking, Systems Practice*, Wiley, London, 1981.

Spray and tree diagrams

2.1 Why spray and tree diagrams?

As explained in the introduction, this book is intended to introduce you to systems analysis techniques which will equip you to work as a computing professional. Whilst most of the described techniques perform a major role within recognized structured analysis approaches, this chapter describes two complementary techniques which play only a small part – for when we reach Chapter 5, you will find that the use of *decision trees* is simply one of several techniques recommended when preparing elementary process descriptions at the most detailed level of data flow diagrams. If none of this means anything to you yet, don't worry – it will. In this chapter, however, we give tree diagrams more prominence than they would seem to merit. So why are we doing this? The reason is that the use of tree diagrams in a wider context can assist greatly in the organization and structure of information. Their use is often preceded by spray diagrams, as these assist in the relevant information being captured in the first place.

Spray and tree diagrams are therefore two different techniques, but complement each other and are frequently used together. They work in the same way that our own thought processes do: first capturing information, then organizing it. We do this all the time. A simple example would be the planning of a shopping trip. We could first make a list of what was needed; we would be capturing the relevant information. We could then decide the most efficient way of visiting the appropriate shops; we would now be analysing and organizing the captured information. Whether we plan shopping trips by writing lists or simply by remembering what we need to buy will depend upon how many items we need to purchase, and how good our memories are. The principle however remains the same. We capture the information, then organize it.

Spray and tree diagrams can act as a great 'personal tool' between, say, analysts in a team. An individual analyst can use the technique to sort out ideas, and then communicate them in a clear and structured way to colleagues. Or a spray diagram can be created from a group 'brain storming' session, and then various tree diagrams created to show alternative structured views of the captured facts.

Spray and tree diagrams are also a useful study skill, as they can assist greatly in the learning of new concepts and techniques. They have many other uses. Time spent on this chapter will undoubtedly pay dividends later. We begin with spray diagrams.

2.2 Spray diagrams (the 'controlled brain-storm')

These are sometimes called *scatter* diagrams – or even *egg* diagrams. As explained above, they allow for the initial recording of the relevant information, i.e. data *capture*. They also assist in the transition from disorganized facts into structured analysis. To try one out, in the middle of a piece of paper write the title of a main subject to be analysed – try *transport* to begin with – and draw a circle around it (or an ellipse, from which the egg diagram gets its name). Now think of anything you can which is even remotely associated with the subject (e.g. *cars*, *buses*, *fares*, *airports*). As you think of each item, write it on the paper around the centre subject title, connecting each to the subject with a line. The example in Figure 2.1 is by no means complete, but use it as a basis and try to come up with as many entries as you can within five minutes or so. By formalizing data capture in this way, it is often surprising how much information can be gathered in a short time.

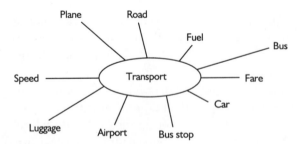

Figure 2.1   Basic spray diagram

When everything to do with the subject has been entered on the sheet, the entries should be examined for *relationships*, and roughly grouped together – see Figure 2.2.

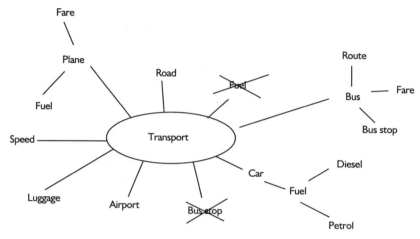

Figure 2.2   Spray diagram being developed

Fare has been placed beside *bus* and *plane*, but not beside *car*. The diagram is now forcing you to *analyse* and helping you begin to *organize* the captured information.

You will find that this process often leads you to think of other entries and relationships overlooked during the first phase. In this example *diesel* and *petrol* have been introduced as sub-groups of *fuel*, and *route* has been introduced and related to *bus*. *Bus stop* and *fuel* have been crossed out, because they have become sub-groups of other items.

Introducing another item can radically change the diagram. If *road transport* was an item, *cars* and *buses* could be linked with it and perhaps *bicycles* then introduced and related. If *motorized transport* was specified however, only *cars* and *buses* would be part of this. You may like to reproduce the basic diagram above, adding other items and changing the structure as described.

Spray diagrams always end up a bit of a mess, with lots of crossings out as relationships are refined – but they carry out data *capture*, *analysis* and to an extent *organization*, effectively. The relationships now have to be further refined and presented neatly, in order to complete the organization and then *communicate* it.

2.3 Tree diagrams

2.3.1 Drawing one

As mentioned earlier, tree diagrams are often used within systems analysis for illustrating decision making, and as such are referred to as *decision trees*. Whilst their recognized role within systems analysis is often confined to describing detailed decision processes (more about this in Chapter 5), they are useful for much more than this.

Continuing with the above example, the main subject – in this case *transport* – is now written at the *left* of the sheet, half way down. By now copying and/or refining the items and relationships from the spray diagram, a simple graphic representation emerges of whatever was being analysed in the first place (see Figure 2.3). As relationships are noted, it will be seen that groups and sub-groups are established – or even sub-sub groups – and these can be shown using *branching* lines. The important thing is that anyone should be able to understand it.

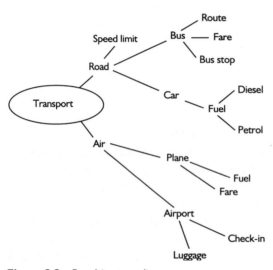

Figure 2.3   Resulting tree diagram

Sometimes it is tempting to create a tree diagram directly, without the spray diagram first, but this usually demands a re-draw anyway, to neaten things up. There are no hard-and-fast rules, however, as long as you end up with a tree diagram which includes all of the relevant items and relationships, you have *captured* the relevant facts, *analysed* them, *organized* them, and *communicated* your findings. It may even be that you are simply communicating your findings to yourself. If, for instance, the above exercise had been carried out because you needed to write a report about transport, the structure of the main body of the report would now be based upon the derived tree diagram (see Figure 2.4).

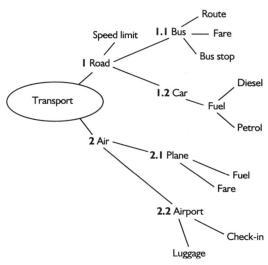

Figure 2.4 Tree diagram as a basis for a report

2.3.2 More tree diagram applications

As a systems analyst you will often need to interview users, or attend conferences, presentations and meetings. From now on, instead of taking 'normal' notes make a spray diagram of all the main points and associations – with the key subject in the middle. Afterwards, draw the tree diagram. If you become particularly adept at these, or the talk is nicely constructed, you can create the tree diagram directly. In either case, you will now have a structured summary. If you are a student and have used lectures as your basis you will have a great 'revision aid' for the topic, to be used alongside handouts and textbooks.

Even such written information can however benefit from the tree diagram treatment. If you have a handout or text book chapter which you are finding difficult, make a tree diagram of it. You can even make a 'high level' tree diagram of a whole book or subject area. If you are trying to find out as much as possible about a particular subject, using a number of books all at once, capture what you read on to a spray diagram: you will then have a 'distilled' version of everything *all* of the books have told you – on one diagram. Turn it into a tree diagram and the facts will gain structure and be much easier to understand. Drawing it will in itself help you understand, and using it will help you revise.

The diagram below (Figure 2.5) shows the beginnings of a tree diagram illustrating the structure of three SSADM techniques. Even if you know nothing about the subject yet, the diagram communicates the structure and terminology in a clear and unambiguous way. As you continue through this book it may be an idea to return to the illustration occasionally, hopefully seeing it make an increasing amount of sense.

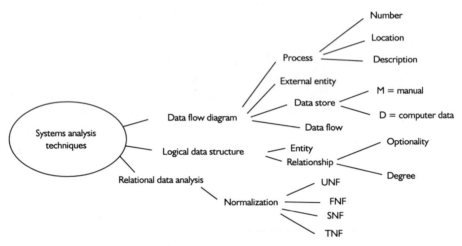

Figure 2.5   Tree diagram of systems analysis techniques

Spray and tree diagrams can help you plan a talk, design a system-menu structure, draw up a questionnaire, prepare an interview or plan a project. You may well begin to wonder how you previously managed without them!

Look at the simple examples which follow – they have deliberately been left a little short on detail so that you can see if you can add more to them. They are based upon the idea that you work for a software house and are involved in organizing a small project team in responding to an invitation to tender.

First, the whole project would need to be organized (Figure 2.6), and then the software to be used in the development of a system would need to be chosen (Figure 2.7) and perhaps a presentation planned (Figure 2.8). More examples could obviously be shown, but we hope that these figures will give you the idea.

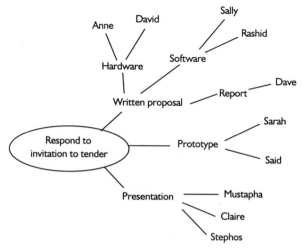

Figure 2.6   Tree diagram showing organization of a project

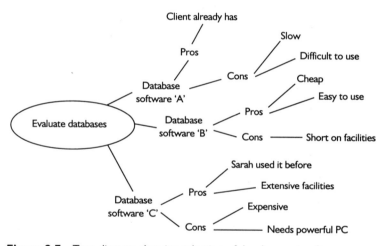

Figure 2.7   Tree diagram showing selection of development software

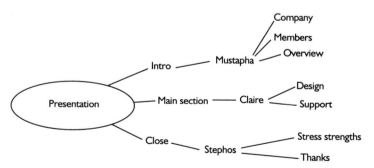

Figure 2.8   Tree diagram showing organization of a presentation session

Summary

This chapter began with a rationale for the spray and tree diagram approach. It then used a simple example to demonstrate the technique, and showed a number of further instances appropriate to the world of information systems. We hope that you have found the chapter useful. With spray and tree diagrams behind you, it should be possible to approach the rest of this book in a structured, efficient way, as you discover more powerful structured analysis techniques. The less time you need to spend learning about these techniques, and therefore the sooner you can begin to put them into practice, the better. A tree diagram 'summary' of each chapter could be a useful way to reduce learning time.

Further reading

K. Williams, *Study Skills*, Chapter 2, Macmillan, London, 1989.

3

Introducing Data Flow Diagrams (DFDs)

3.1 Physical and logical views

It is always possible to view a circumstance in two basic ways – physically and logically. We actually do it often, but probably never think about it. As we continue in our discovery of systems analysis it is a great help to recognize this innate ability that we all have.

The people in a room may, for instance, easily be identified by a physical characteristic such as hair colour, or those who are wearing jumpers or not. It would then be simple to create a tree diagram combining these groupings (see Figure 3.1), thus representing one *logical interpretation* of the *physical fact* that there was a variety of people in the room.

It would be just as simple, however, to create a tree diagram showing marital status, qualifications, likes and dislikes, whether the person was a parent or not – or, if a classroom situation, whether a lecturer or student. This would again represent a *logical* view, but this time based upon characteristics which could be said to be not really physical at all, or at least less physically obvious. The successful 'unravelling' of facts by logical interpretation is a basic requirement of systems analysis. One of the advantages of tree diagramming is that it allows both views to be taken. These can either be separated as described, or combined. It would be possible to divide all people wearing jumpers into those who are married or not.

How about a row of apparently identical buses at a bus stop? Almost without thinking, we know that there is, we hope, an important difference between them, i.e. they have different numbers and therefore different destinations. The *physical* view

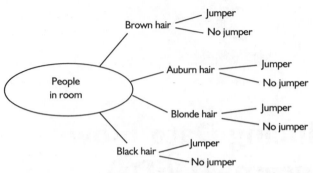

Figure 3.1   Tree diagram showing groupings of people in a room

identifies them as all being red, all at the same bus stop, whereas the *logical* view highlights the important piece of information that makes the difference. Let us now imagine, however, that one is a minibus, one a single decker and another a double decker, but that all have the *same* number. Assuming that your objective is to get home, you will simply choose the one at the front of the queue, i.e. ignoring the *physical* view, and taking the *logical* one. Let us take this example a little further. It is now time for all three buses to have their service, and they are parked in the maintenance shed. The mechanic cares little which destination number is displayed on the front of each – what *he* finds important is that one is a Volvo, one a Mercedes and one a DAF. He is applying the information which is relevant to him, to a physical situation, and arriving at a logical conclusion – in this case indentifying the differing service requirements.

Consider a situation in which you wish to communicate with a friend. If the friend is sitting next to you, you simply speak. If you and your friend are at your respective homes you can telephone, or write. These are different *physical* situations, but in one respect could be said to result in the same *logical* happening, i.e. you communicate with your friend.

The key point in the above is that the logical view depends upon the *relevant information*. Because business information systems are all to do with information, it is important that the difference between the two views is seen clearly. More than this, however, business systems involve the *transfer* and *processing* of information. Analysis of a business situation usually begins with identification and analysis of all *documents* involved, i.e. the physical view, followed by analysis of the *data* which they contain, i.e. the logical view.

3.2 Document flow diagrams

The diagramming technique which is used to identify the physical movement of documents is a very simple one, and is called *document* flow diagramming. A technique called *data* flow diagramming is then utilized, to handle the transformation from physical document to logical data – more of this later. Document flow diagramming is the first major *official* technique which needs to be learned by the new systems analyst. It depicts where the document comes from, where it goes to and what it is called. The *source* and *destination* of the document are commonly called *agencies*, and these are usually depicted using an *elliptical* shape.

In the case of the letter to your friend, you and your friend are both agencies and the letter is the document which *flows* from one to the other, as shown in Figure 3.2.

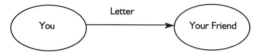

Figure 3.2   A first document flow diagram

In business, the agencies will typically be departments within a company or outside contacts with the company, e.g. a purchase order may be sent from the purchasing department to a supplier. The supplier may deliver the goods to the stores complete with a delivery note, and send an invoice to the purchasing department. The document flow diagram would look like Figure 3.3.

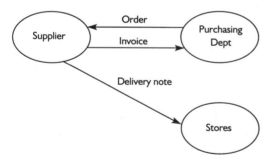

Figure 3.3   Document flow diagram of purchasing system

Document flow diagrams can often prove useful in identifying 'high level' inconsistencies/omissions. You may like to examine the above diagram carefully, and read again the short system description that preceded it. Think about what is going on, and decide whether the addition of one more document flow would 'tighten up' the administration of the depicted system. First, try to do so without looking at the solution in Figure 3.4.

It can be seen that if the stores were to pass the delivery note back to the

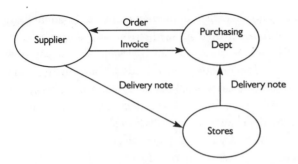

Figure 3.4   Document flow diagram of purchasing system – enhanced

purchasing department, this department would have automatic confirmation of the validity, or otherwise, of the invoice received from the supplier. We hope that you managed to work this out and found that the diagram helped more than the text, for if so the diagram did its job. It communicated the analysis that had originally taken place, made it easier to identify a shortcoming in the system and, finally, allowed for the clear communication of a means of correcting it.

3.3 Data Flow Diagrams (DFDs)

3.3.1 What they are

So we have discovered a useful diagramming technique for depicting how a system works, in terms of the documents that it uses. Documents are, however, simply a convenient way of carrying data in a form which is easily accessible to humans, and advances in technology mean that electronic means are increasingly supplementing the paper-based ones. It is the data which is important – what it is, where it comes from, where it goes. The technique which allows us to discover this data is called data flow diagramming.

Data flow diagrams are one of the most powerful and useful techniques available to the systems analyst. In the development of a new or enhanced computer-based system they are the interface between what is happening in the 'real world' of day-to-day business, and how these activities can be converted into suitable software. DFDs can be used not only to highlight procedural shortcomings, but also to recommend a system structure which will overcome them. The transformation from current inefficiency to future improvement is done in a series of steps that involve the 'unravelling' of what is *logically* happening within what is *physically perceived* to be happening. Using data flow diagrams to create this transformation is not only extremely useful, but is also quite easy; yet there are many badly designed systems around simply because the analyst failed to appreciate this. A new system created without going through the logicalization process will inevitably incorporate many of the shortcomings of the old one, and a brilliantly *logicalized* DFD based upon a poor physical one will simply be built upon a weak foundation. Both stages are therefore equally important.

3.3.2 A simple DFD

There is virtually no situation where a data flow diagram cannot be used to describe a circumstance. At present you are reading this book. You are indulging in an activity, carrying out a *process* which we hope involves assimilating the data you are reading. The book is merely a convenient way of holding this data – it is a *datastore*. You could do various things with this assimilated data – perhaps simply tell a friend what you have learned. This friend would be seen as an *external entity*. A data flow diagram would look something like the one in Figure 3.5, joining the process to the datastore and external entity using *data flows* which depict what data is flowing, and its direction. In order to describe this one activity, the four main elements of data flow diagrams are illustrated, i.e. process, datastore, external entity and data flow.

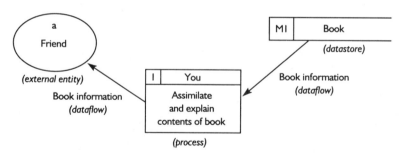

Figure 3.5   A first data flow diagram

Let us return briefly to the example of your communication with your friend. The document flow diagram was only capable of showing the instance where you sent your friend a letter, but because all three versions of your communication involved the transfer of data, the data flow diagram can show all three (see Figure 3.6).

These examples are called *physical* DFDs, Figure 3.6 depicting three physical

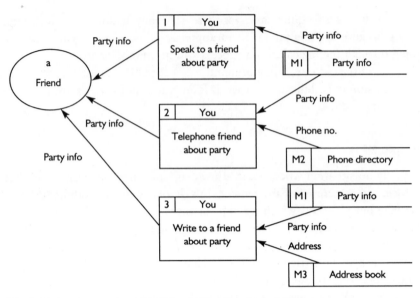

Figure 3.6   Communicating with your friend – physical DFD.

happenings – i.e. we have in DFD terms *processes*. In Figure 3.7, however, is a first look at the way in which DFDs can alternatively be used to show the *logical* view of a situation, representing the same events but without any physical constraints.

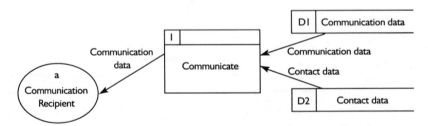

Figure 3.7   Communicating with your friend – logical DFD

It now does not matter to the 'system' that it is you who is communicating, or that it is your friend who receives the communication, or even that the communication is about a party – but it would still allow all activities shown in the physical DFD to take place.

Before you can begin to create your own DFDs like those above, it is necessary to have a more detailed look at the notation that we have been using.

3.3.3 DFD notation

Introducing the four elements

There are many conventions for drawing data flow diagrams, but they all depict in one way or another the four elements above, i.e.:

- movement of data (*data flows* – arrows show direction, 'labels' indicate the data which is flowing – e.g. 'stock details', 'supplier details');
- *processes* which make the data flow (e.g. 'issue stock');
- *data stores* within the system (e.g. a filing cabinet, card index, or computer file);
- sources or destinations of data outside the system (often termed *external entities*, e.g. a customer, or supplier, or other department).

Some also allow for *physical resource flows* (e.g. a movement of goods).

The different elements of the data flow diagram are specified below. Do not be put off if it all sounds difficult at this stage – everything should become clear as we work through an example later in the chapter. For the time being, read through the details which follow, assuming that you will refer back to them on several occasions as you learn more.

A *data flow* is shown by a line with an arrowhead, indicating the direction of flow (see Figure 3.8). Each *data flow* must have a *label* to explain what it is. Note that no *alteration* of data can take place within a flow line.

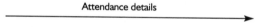

Attendance details

Figure 3.8   A DFD *data flow*

A *process* is the only part of the DFD that portrays something actually happening, including any decisions that are made. Each process consists of a rectangle as shown (Figure 3.9): the small left hand box contains the process *number*; to the right is entered the process *location* – a *person* or a *place* (i.e. which person or department *causes* the happening); the main box contains the process *description* (*what* is happening).

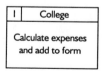

Figure 3.9   A DFD *process*

Data cannot be created or destroyed as a result of a process, i.e. what comes in should go out. Note that the description within a process box must start with an *imperative verb*, e.g. Calculate net pay, Accumulate totals. The number of processes on a DFD should not normally exceed seven or so. If it does, the DFD should be reviewed and certain functions combined into one function. Further *levels* of a diagram are created to reveal the extra detail – we'll come to this later.

An open-ended rectangle indicates a *data store* – see Figure 3.10. In the small left box is entered a reference of 'D' (computer-held data) or 'M' (manually held data) followed by the *data store number*. If it is necessary (for the purposes of a neat layout) to show the same data store more than once on a diagram, all instances of it should have a *duplicate* line added, as in the example on the right.

Figure 3.10   DFD *data stores*: (a) data store *single* occurrence; (b) data store *multiple* occurrence

An ellipse indicates an *external entity* – see Figure 3.11. This is defined as a source or destination of data outside of the system. It could, for instance, be a person, a group of people, a department, or a whole company. The entity *description* is entered within the ellipse, together with the entity *reference*. If it is necessary (for the purposes of a neat layout) to show the same external entity more than once on a diagram, all instances of it should have a *duplicate* line added, as in the example on the right of Figure 3.11.

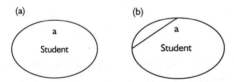

Figure 3.11   DFD *external entities*: (a) external entity *single* occurrence; (b) external entity *multiple* occurrence

A broad arrow represents a *physical resource flow*, e.g. a movement of goods – see Figure 3.12. This symbol is the least common one, and is in any instance only used in *physical* DFDs. The *resource name* is entered inside the arrow.

Figure 3.12   A DFD *resource flow*

It is worth spending a moment clarifying the use of these, as students tend to either ignore them altogether or use them when they should not. There is actually a separate technique known as *resource flow diagramming*, where such flows are given great importance. Within DFDs, however, their use is much more secondary, such flows only being shown if they trigger a movement of data, whilst not themselves being accompanied by data. Perhaps the most common example is a successful delivery of goods to a customer which triggers the sending of an invoice. If the goods were accompanied by a delivery note the physical resource flow would not be shown because it would be the delivery note which was the carrier of data, and thus a conventional data flow would be used.

DFD 'levelling'

One of the main requirements of preparing successful data flow diagrams is that of deciding how much detail to show. It is entirely within your control at any stage of the analysis process. Data flow diagrams are expanded (or *decomposed*) into *levels* – uncovering more and more detail by separating each process into sub-processes, then sub-sub-processes and so on. Students often struggle with the concepts being described here – in particular, how to tell whether a dataflow diagram is a level 1, or level 2, and so on. If you are finding it somewhat difficult there is no need to worry, it will all become clear.

The highest 'real' data flow diagram level, which utilizes the four elements described in Section 3.3.3, is level 1. In practice, this 'highest' level is decided by *you*! You simply draw a dataflow diagram which depicts a required set of circumstances, using no more than five or so process boxes (this is a sensible maximum, at least to start with). This is your 'level 1 DFD'. The level *above*, i.e. 'level 0', is your context diagram and consists of one process box with an overall description which covers the activities on your level 1 DFD. The next *lower* level which you draw will be level 2 and will consist of one DFD for each level 1 process, each showing that process further broken down. The level below that, level 3, will have the sub-processess broken down into sub-sub-processes. The lowest level is reached when it is impossible to decompose processes any further, and consists of detailed descriptions called *Elementary Process Descriptions* (EPDs) – commonly utilizing decision trees, or decision tables, or structured English. The means of achieving all of this will be explained in the next chapter, but to help with the concept it is worth studying Figure 3.13.

Whilst there are no rules regarding the number of levels of DFD which can be used, level 3 is commonly the lowest required. Each process within the boundary of the lower level DFD is identified by a decimal extension of the higher level identifier. The first important point is that a process box at a higher level becomes the DFD

Dataflow diagram *levels* ...

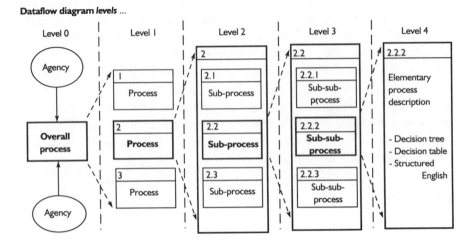

... providing progressive **decomposition** *of processes, until* **elementary** *process description* **level is reached.**

Figure 3.13 DFD levelling

boundary for the lower level, and there must be consistency between DFD levels, with all the data going in or out of a DFD appearing on the higher level DFD. If a data store is used only for that one process, it is placed within the boundary of that process, whilst a data store used by other processes is placed outside the boundary. External entities are, however, always shown as being outside the boundary of a lower level process, even if they communicate only with that process.

EPDs complete the bottom level of a set of DFDs by stating the policy and procedure for converting input data flows to output data flows. They provide details of the logic of bottom level DFD processes. As explained earlier, they can be written in various ways – structured English, decision trees, decision tables, or other methods, including narrative or flowcharts.

You may feel that some of the above is quite difficult to understand. If so, everything should become clearer as you read on.

3.3.4 From documents to data

Where to begin

The data flow diagrams seen so far may have seemed simple, but the means of developing the technique further, including the 'levelling' concept, may initially confuse you. You may be wondering where you would begin if faced with the need to analyse the processes going on within a whole company. You will see later that it simply entails tackling the business problem in straightforward stages, thus creating data flow diagrams that are clear and extremely useful.

For the moment, however, we are concentrating upon having you appreciate the *concepts* of DFDs, rather than how to analyse a full-blown business situation. Let us start with something that everyone understands – the documents that the company uses. Because documents are physical they can be seen, handled, discussed and analysed. Remember, they are simply a convenient way of carrying data, and it is the data we are interested in.

Whilst it is not only documents which carry data, consideration of other means of communicating data to humans can come later. For the present, it important to note only that document flows and data flows are inextricably linked. Once a document flow diagram has been established, the processes that are going on inside it can be 'discovered' using a straightforward technique, which also unearths the datastores and external entities involved, thus creating the data flow diagram.

The document flow diagram

Imagine that you are in a helicopter, hovering above an industrial estate. You have a pair of zoom binoculars with special lenses which, when focused upon a particular company, show you all of the departments – and even the customers and suppliers that the company deals with – laid out as a great big document flow diagram! You zoom in further and concentrate upon the factory area of the company. You see the diagram shown in Figure 3.14. Do not worry if you cannot visualize what some of the documents are – all you need to appreciate is that *documents* are moving between *agencies*.

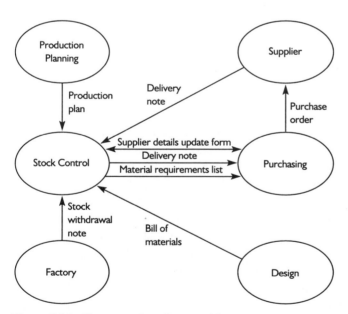

Figure 3.14 Document flow diagram of factory area

The context diagram

You now move the binoculars until the stock control department is in the centre of your view. Magically, the shape of this department changes into a rectangle, and at the same time you notice that the purchase order document flow has disappeared. The diagram you are now looking at (Figure 3.15) is called a context diagram, because it shows one department in context, i.e. ignoring any document flows which occur between other departments. In this case the purchase order has gone because it only flowed between purchasing and the supplier.

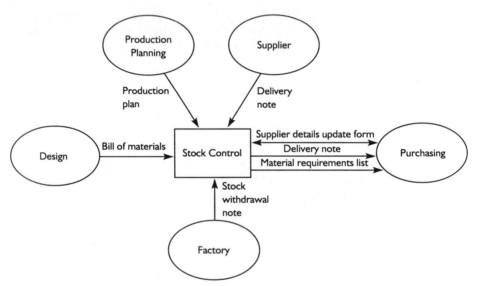

Figure 3.15   Context diagram of stock control

The data flow diagram

We can zoom in even further, however. Blank documents are useless pieces of paper, and there is of course something printed on these documents – data. It is really the *data* which flows between departments and between people, and it is procedures, or *processes*, which make it flow. Computers do not process documents, they process data. This is where data flow diagrams come in – the context diagram in Figure 3.15 can also be viewed as a *level 0 data flow diagram*. One small change makes this clear, i.e. by adding a process description to the stock control box, as in Figure 3.16.

Note that a level 0 data flow diagram is not quite a *real* data flow diagram in that it does not incorporate any datastores, and because there is only one process box it does not have a number. SSADM-style referencing has, however, been added to the external entities. To clarify the stage we have reached see Figure 3.17, which has been 'laid out'

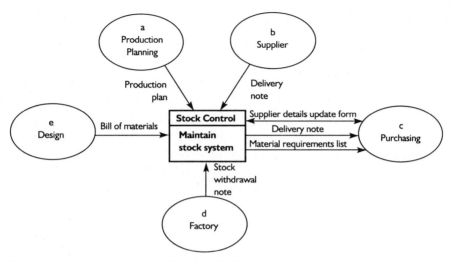

Figure 3.16   Stock control level 0 physical DFD

to match the original example that depicted you reading this book. For convenience, the original is reproduced bottom right.

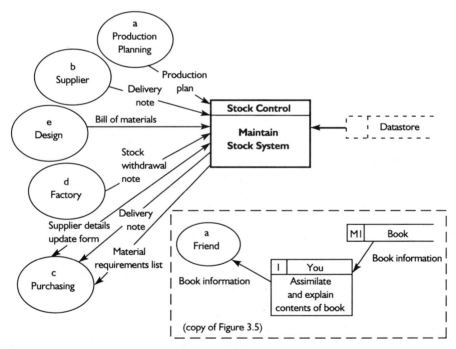

Figure 3.17   Stock control level 0 physical DFD – modified layout

Whilst datastores are not shown at level *0*, a *notional* one has been included in the above example to make comparison easier. One of the key benefits of going on to expand to more detailed levels is the fact that you are forced to consider what data is needed to support the identified processes. You could hardly tell your friend what you had read in the book without having the book as a *datastore* to provide the information to you in the first place. In the stock control example, the next step is to look at the different processes which together make up the overall stock control function, and as a result discover the manual files, card indexes etc. that support it. We will now complete a level 1 DFD of the above stock control system, just to give you the idea.

Imagine that, as an analyst, you have spoken with the people who carry out the stock control functions and discovered more about what goes on within the department. You may well draw a DFD in the stages detailed below. When creating DFDs it is always best to concentrate first upon the processes, then identify the datastores and external entities, and finally add the data flows. It is also useful when first starting to draw DFDs to get into a habit of entering the processes down the middle of the page, with external entities then added to the left and datastores to the right. This encourages a step-by-step approach and tends to result in diagrams which are better laid out and easier to read, as illustrated below.

Note first the processes (Figure 3.18), followed by the data stores and external entities (Figure 3.19), and finally the data flows (Figure 3.20).

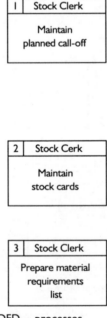

Figure 3.18   Stock control level 1 DFD – processes

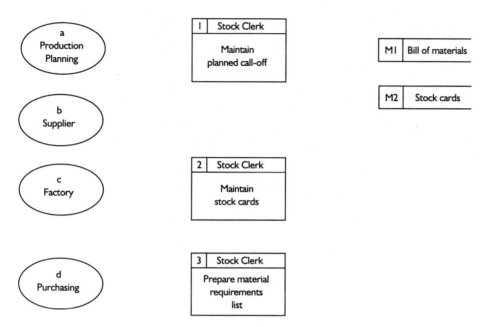

Figure 3.19   Stock control level I physical DFD – processes, datastores and external entities

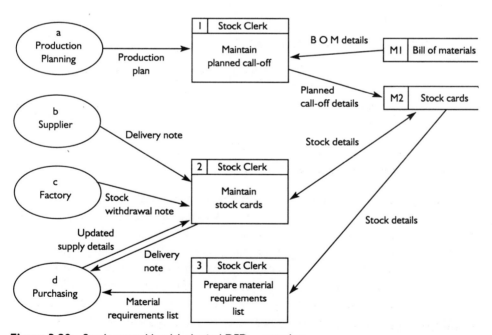

Figure 3.20   Stock control level I physical DFD – complete

The diagram thus created – i.e. a level 1 DFD – gives a good overall idea of what happens within the stock control function, and this may well be all that is required. In the same way that the overall process of the level 0 DFD led to the discovery of a number of level 1 processes, however, each of these level 1 processes can in turn be expanded further to reveal a greater degree of detail, – thus revealing the sub-processes which take place at the more detailed level, as explained in the section *DFD levelling.* Let us consider process 3 *Prepare material requirements list.* What exactly is happening here? It could well be as shown in Figure 3.21.

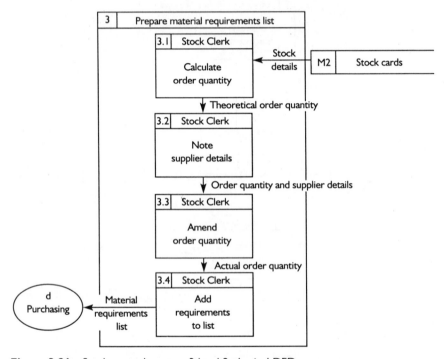

Figure 3.21   Stock control process 3 level 2 physical DFD

Do not be too concerned if you haven't got the hang of all the DFD notation yet: there will be plenty of opportunity for this as we practice the creation of DFDs in the next chapter. It is also fairly unlikely that you know enough about stock control systems to be able to work out sensible sub-processes. We are simply endeavouring to illustrate some DFD principles at present, and hope that you are at least beginning to get the idea. DFDs are so important within systems analysis that we are trying to approach them in different ways to ensure that you understand them. The greater variety you see, the more you will get used to reading them. Because of this, the chapter ends with a look at another couple of examples.

3.4 Two more examples of DFDs

3.4.1 The hairdressing salon

Take a look at the following level 1 DFD (Figure 3.22) and simply see whether you

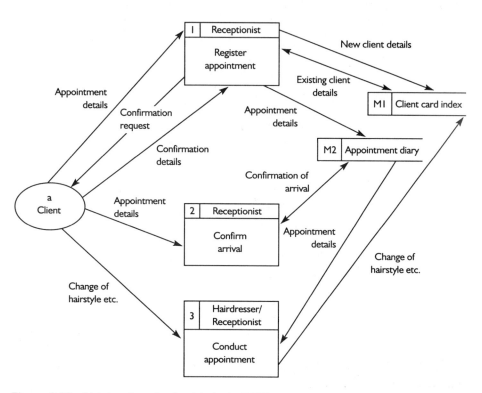

Figure 3.22   Hairdressing salon level 1 physical DFD

can understand what it is trying to tell you. If so, it should further convince you how useful DFDs can be as an analysis and communication tool – you have only just been introduced to them and already it should be pretty evident what is going on in the example. It is of course possible to draw DFDs which are confusing and difficult to read, but if you get used to reading examples which are clear, you are more likely to create clear ones of your own.

The level 1 DFD processes shown could be further expanded into sub-processes in the same way as was shown with the stock control system. Let us look at *conduct appointment*. This is an interesting process because two people in the salon are involved in it, i.e. the hairdresser and the receptionist. By expanding it into sub-processes we discover who contributes what – see Figure 3.23.

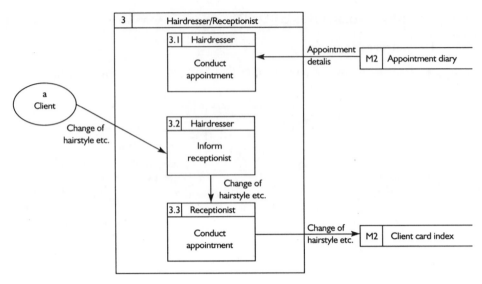

Figure 3.23   Hairdressing salon process 3 level 2 physical DFD

3.4.2 The integrated accounting system

Finally, here is a comparison between a standard block diagram of an integrated accounting system – similar to the kind found in many text books used on accountancy courses – and a DFD of the same system. The block diagram is an excellent one of its type, and gives a good idea of the major components of the system. The systems analyst would need to know much more, however, and this is where the DFD comes into its own.

Whilst you will find that the block diagram (Figure 3.24) is obviously simpler, the information which the DFD (Figure 3.25) contains is far more detailed and communicative. It tells you how the system *works*, rather than simply the elements it consists of.

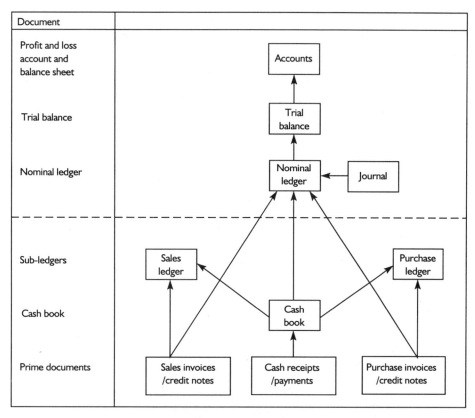

Figure 3.24 Integrated accounting system block diagram (from G. Taylor, *Computer Studies GCSE* (3rd edn), p. 164. Macmillan, New York, 1991)

Summary

This chapter began by introducing the concept of taking either a purely physical view or a logical view of a circumstance. It then showed how the physical view, as depicted by the movement of documents within a system, can be communicated using the document flow diagramming technique. We then saw that documents exist only for the purpose of carrying data, and have ended by introducing one of the most useful ways of diagramming what is going on, i.e. data flow diagrams (DFDs). We hope you feel that you have gained a lot from this chapter. You may wish to go over it again and see how far you have come. Because of the importance of DFDs, the next chapter continues with them – showing by detailed example how to go about creating your own.

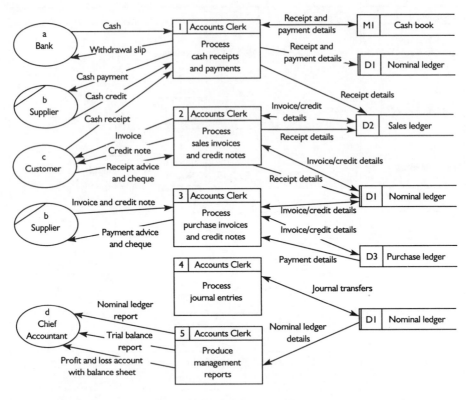

Figure 3.25   An integrated accounting system level I DFD

Further reading

C. Britton and J. Doake, *Software System Development – a Gentle Introduction*, Chapter 3, McGraw-Hill, London, 1993.

Creating DFDs

4.1 From theory to practice

4.1.1 Unreal and artificial

So far, we have seen why we need DFDs, the symbols used in their construction, the fundamental idea of different levels, and a number of examples. It is now time to try a couple. Before we start, however, we would just like to point out a serious problem we have when writing about DFDs for you as an aspiring systems analyst – the fact that it is all a bit unreal, or artificial.

There are two reasons for this. First, when we as authors are writing about a technique, we have to think of a scenario or example which we can use to illustrate the development of that technique. We therefore invent one, or use one from our own experience, and write it down on paper so that readers can use it to draw, say, a data flow diagram. The unfortunate thing with this is that nearly all the work has already been done, in producing the scenario.

The really interesting part of systems analysis is in finding out what goes on in the existing system, and to do this you have to interview people, observe procedures, read documents, do some measurements and basically fact-find. To be successful at this, you need all sorts of characteristics other than the ability to draw a data flow diagram – skills like interviewing technique, diplomacy, attention to detail, patience etc. It is virtually impossible to learn these aspects of systems analysis from a book – you need to go on courses which involve role play and simulation, actively practise systems analysis and watch an experienced systems analyst in action. The drawing of the DFD is probably the *least* important part of the initial systems investigation – the really important part is getting the facts right and establishing a rapport with your users. The DFD is simply a tool which you use to describe what you have found, as well as being a good communication tool in its own right.

4.1.2 Context diagrams in context

The second reason is inextricably linked with the first. You may have got the impression from the previous chapter that all you need to do with DFDs is to start off with a document flow diagram, change this into a context diagram, expand this into a level 1 DFD and then expand this DFD into lower and lower levels until you are happy you have everything. Although this is one of the best ways of introducing the concepts of DFDs, it may well not be as easy as that in practice. Imagine you have been brought in to an organization to do a systems analysis on the sales order processing system, which is largely manual. How, practically, can you start off the investigation by drawing a context diagram? You will need to know all the documents which go in and out of the system and who sends them and who receives them, and you will need to know this from scratch. Impossible! Basically, you can only interview one person at a time or observe one process at a time and so you will, of necessity, have to start at the detail end, talking to Fred or Nora about what exactly it is they do. Hence, whilst you will keep your eye on the higher level objective of producing an overall context diagram view of the system, you will be able to piece together snippets of the lower level DFDs as you go along, gradually building up the higher level DFDs, noticing inconsistencies and returning periodically to the lower levels. It is rather like completing a jigsaw.

4.1.3 Functional areas and processes

One final word of advice before we start getting serious. Always start off physical DFDs by giving a process box to a *functional area*. For example, if you are investigating a large system made up of several departments, then make each department a level 1 process box. This makes sense, as it is likely you are going to be investigating one department at a time. Then, when you start on level 2 DFDs, make the process boxes correspond to a person or a section in that department. You will see later on that the whole thing becomes unravelled in any case when we logicalize the system. It is during the logicalization process that you spot duplication and inefficiencies and sort them out. But to start with you need to document what actually happens, warts and all.

Example I – the boat building company   45

4.2 Example I – the boat building company

4.2.1 The scenario

The following description is about the way quotations are produced and processed in a firm which builds boats to a customer's specification. The company is called Marine Construction and the description was obtained from interviews with the General Manager who has a good overview of the whole process.

Customers send to Marine Construction a specification of the boat they want built. The Sales Office use this detail to make out a special form, BQI, which includes the customer specification as well as a deadline date for the quote to be ready. The BQI is then sent to the Design Office who produce the drawing and material specifications and send this with a partially complete BQI to the Materials Office. They price up the material needed using their material catalogue and add this detail to the BQI before passing it to the Production Office. Here, the required labour is estimated and, using the labour rates held in the labour rates file, the estimate is added to the BQI. The BQI is now returned, with the drawings and specifications, to the Sales Office who complete it by adding on an appropriate mark-up by reference to the Sales Manager.

Using the now complete BQI two copies of a formal quotation are prepared. One copy is sent to the customer and the other is filed with the BQI and drawing and materials specifications in the quotes file. If and when the customer sends a letter of intent, the relevant BQI, copy of the quote, drawing and materials specifications are retrieved from the quotes file and sent to the order processing system.

4.2.2 An initial attempt at a level I DFD

As we said before, a lot of the interesting work has been done in producing this description in the first place. Your initial attempt at a data flow diagram is bound to be influenced by the way this description is written. When you look at the description, it is written in a sequential manner – it basically follows a BQ1 around the system. Why don't we therefore try to draw a data flow diagram which mirrors this description and see what it looks like. Have a go yourself and then compare your result to the one in Figure 4.1.

4.2.3 Notes on initial attempt

1. The BQ1 is having data added to it all the time so we have called these updates BQ1(1), BQ1(2) ... BQ1(completed).

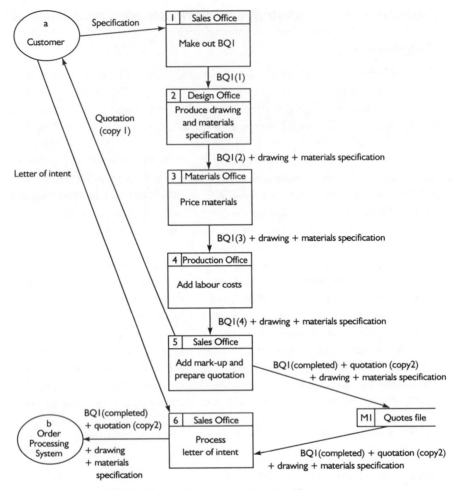

Figure 4.1 Level I DFD for Marine Construction (version I)

2. We have shown documents which are sent together on the same data flows.

3. The only external entities shown are the Customer (this is obvious) and the Order Processing System which is another system within the company and, hence, external to the Quotations System. If we were examining the whole Sales Order Processing System including Quotations, then the Quotations System would itself be a level 1 process box in a much larger DFD.

4. Some of you may have decided that the Sales Manager is an external entity. We have decided he is part of the Sales Office functionality in process box 5 and is

Example I – the boat building company **47**

therefore *part of the action*. You will see when we come on to logicalization that he would probably be made into an external entity later.

5. Note that only one data store is shown on this level 1 DFD – the Quotes File. There are other data stores in the description, but this is the only one used by more than one process. The other data stores belong to one and only one process. At the moment we have not expanded these level 1 boxes into level 2. A data store should only be shown on a DFD if it is used by more than one process at that DFD level. When the processes are expanded further at the next level, the data stores used by the sub-processes are thus exposed. When the level is reached where further expansion is not intended, all further data stores should be shown. This means that if only a level 1 data flow diagram is drawn, then *all* data stores should be shown.

4.2.4 Development of initial attempt

Let us return to the advice we gave in Section 4.1.3, i.e. it was a good idea to make each process box a functional area. It is now time to demonstrate the effect of taking

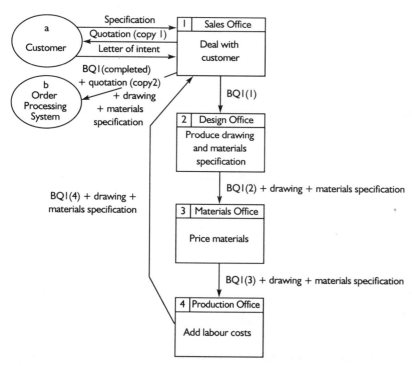

Figure 4.2 Level I DFD for Marine Construction (version 2)

this advice. Have a look again at Figure 4.1 and see if there is anywhere where this is not adhered to.

You should notice that the Design Office, the Materials Office and the Production Office all have their own process boxes, but the Sales Office has three. There is really nothing wrong with this, but our preference would be to combine them into one process box. It is worth remembering that in systems analysis there is rarely a definitive answer! However, our data flow diagram now looks like Figure 4.2.

4.2.5 Explosion of level 1 processes into level 2 processes

Obviously, the initial description of the Marine Construction quotations system was quite high level. We do not know, for example, exactly how the Materials Office and Production Office produce their estimates. However, we probably have enough information about the Sales Office to have a good attempt at a level 2 DFD for this area. The missing information for the Materials and Production Offices is given below. We have not given any further details about the Design Office as this relies heavily on the inspiration, expertise and experience of the designer, and so cannot really be described except to say that they produce the drawing and the materials specification and add some details to the BQ1.

The Materials Office activity takes some care to ensure that accurate costs are produced. Each material specified is checked against the stock card index system. Where sufficient stock is available to fulfil this quotation then the most recent invoice is used for the quote. If there is insufficient stock then the materials catalogue is used.

The Production Office take similar care. The drawing and material specification are used to create a work schedule with each operation of the job identified in terms of equipment used, time taken and labour grade needed. The work schedule is prepared and clipped into a ring binder. Using this work schedule each operation is costed by reference to the labour rates file (a rate depends on the labour grade). In addition, a cost is added depending on the equipment used (by reference to the quarterly cost report) to give a total cost per operation.

The first thing you have to ask is whether it is worth expanding the level 1 boxes into level 2. After all, the descriptions are not that complicated and they could be re-written in a more precise form and act as process descriptions. We always think it is worth having a go, especially when we come to logicalization. When you reach

Example 1 – the boat building company   49

Chapter 8 you will find that having data flow diagrams worked out to a reasonable level of detail really helps the logicalization process.

Our attempts at the level 2 DFDs for the Sales Office, Materials Office and Production Office are in Figures 4.3–4.5.

4.2.6 Notes on level 2 DFDs

1. The asterisk in the bottom right hand corner of a process box indicates that this is a lowest level process and will not be expanded any further.

2. Note the reference numbers of the files M3/1, M3/2 ... M4/1 etc. This is an SSADM convention. M3/1 refers to the first data store in the expansion of process box 3. There is no rule as to which is the first data store, it is normally the one nearest the top of the page. It doesn't really matter as long as each one is uniquely identified. Also, we have shown all the data stores at this level

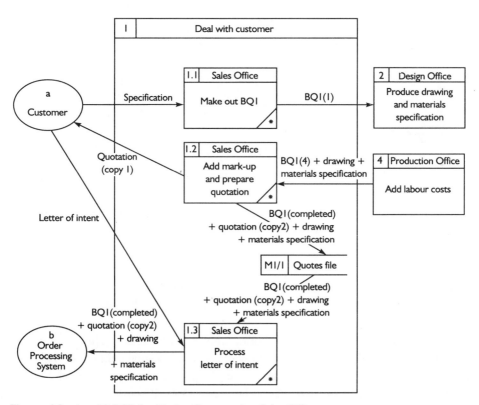

Figure 4.3   Level 2 DFD for Marine Construction Sales Office

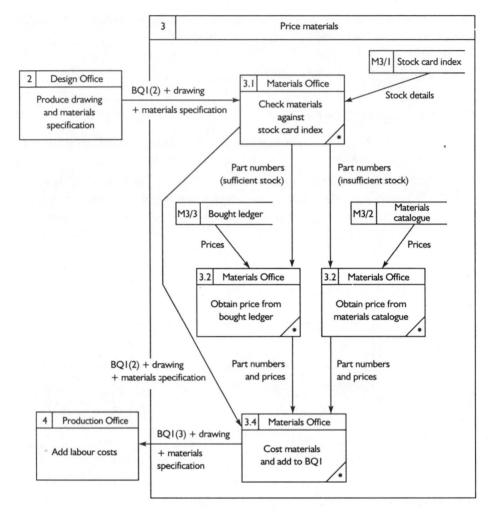

Figure 4.4   Level 2 DFD for Marine Construction Materials Office

regardless of whether they are used by more than one process. This is because we are not going to expand the processes any further, and it is a good idea to show all data stores on a set of DFDs.

3. You may have noticed that DFDs contain no decision symbol. This is one clear way in which they are different to flow charts, and is quite deliberate. Any decisions which are made are described in the process description which accompanies each of the lowest level DFD processes. Process 3.1 in the Materials Office will, for instance, involve a decision as to whether there is

Example 1 – the boat building company   51

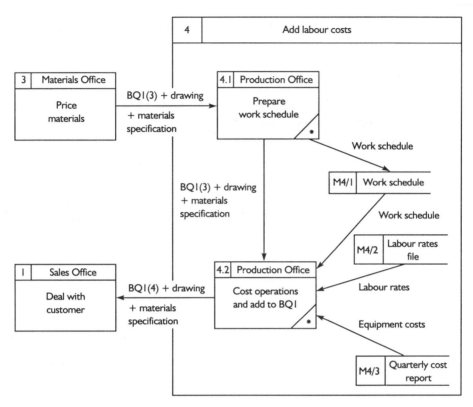

Figure 4.5   Level 2 DFD for Marine Construction Production Office

sufficient stock of a material to meet the estimate. This is implied by the two data flows coming out of 3.1 called Part numbers (sufficient stock) and Part numbers (insufficient stock). The data on both flows is exactly the same – it is a list of part numbers, but the bracketed part is there to add meaning to the data flow diagram. Data flow diagrams are, after all, intended to act as a communication tool.

4. You should notice that all three level 2 DFDs are *consistent* with the level 1 DFD. In other words, all the data going into and out from each level 1 process box must also go into and out from the level 2 expansion of that process. You cannot suddenly introduce or lose data flows, as this would lead to uncertainty and inconsistency. Around the outside of the level 2 processes you should see all the external entities and other processes and data stores which feed data into and receive data from the process.

4.3 Example 2 – the student assessment system

4.3.1 The scenario

The following example is about the system used to assess students on the second year of a degree course in business computing. The system was used in our university until a couple of years ago, and we have chosen it because it is fairly straightforward and yet has sufficient subtle little touches to make it interesting. We have simplified it slightly for the sake of clarity.

Students study six subjects

quantitative methods;

systems analysis and design;

computer systems;

software engineering;

business studies;

behavioural studies.

They are assessed in each subject by coursework and an end-of-year examination. The following description of the system is based around the roles of the various *players* in the system.

The Subject Tutor

Subject Tutors first get involved when they are allocated to a subject by the timetabler. Subject Tutors are responsible for setting coursework (assignments) and giving them to students. The student completes the assignment and returns it to the Subject Tutor. They are then marked, the marks recorded and the assignments returned to the students with feedback. There may be a number of assignments per subject, each with a different weighting (i.e. some assignments may be worth 50 per cent of the coursework mark, while others only 20 per cent). Tutors record the marks in a variety of ways. Most use a spreadsheet while some still record them on paper. At the end of the year the Subject Tutor must calculate a final coursework mark for each student and pass a copy of these to the Year Leader.

Subject Tutors are also responsible for setting an end-of-year examination. Once the paper is written and moderated (we shall ignore the moderation process for simplicity) the paper is sent to the Examinations Office who organize the time and place of the examination, arrange for the exam to be invigilated and then return the completed scripts to the subject tutor. The Subject Tutor then marks the scripts, records the mark and sends a copy to the Year Leader along with the coursework marks.

Example 2 – the student assessment system   53

The Year Leader

The Year Leader is responsible for the final collation of marks for presentation to the Board of Examiners. The Year Leader produces a spreadsheet which shows, for each student, the coursework mark and the examination mark for each subject and the weighted average of these two marks (courseworks and examinations normally have a 20:80 per cent weighting). Any fails are highlighted on the spreadsheet and the Year Leader brings copies of the spreadsheet to the Board of Examiners, together with any mitigating evidence received from the student.

The Board of Examiners

The Board is made up of all the Subject Tutors, the Year Leader (who is almost always a Subject Tutor as well) and at least one external examiner, and is chaired by the Director of School. The School Administrator is also in attendance to record decisions and take minutes. The Board looks at each student's marks carefully, takes into consideration any mitigating evidence and decides on the results for each student by applying a set of regulations. The regulations are complicated and will not be described here, but basically students may be required to do extra work in some subjects or, in extreme cases, may have to repeat the whole year or even withdraw from the course.

The School Administrator

When the School Administrator receives the results from the Board of Examiners, she produces a pass list which she passes to the Head of School. The results are then filed in a course results file. The Head of School signs the pass list and returns it to the School Administrator who files it with the results. When all the results from all of the Boards of Examiners have been processed in this way, the School Administrator sends a copy of the results and pass list to the Examinations Office.

Students who wish to have a copy of the results must submit a stamped addressed envelope to the School Administrator who sets up a file of such envelopes. A little while after the Board of Examiners, the School Administrator matches the results to the names on the envelopes and sends the results to the students.

4.3.2 Initial discussion

This description is very different to the one for Marine Construction. Have a close look at the two to see what the basic difference is.

Yes, this one is already broken down into functional areas. The Marine Construction description is very sequential – one thing happens after another. This one is different – it concentrates on the jobs performed by the various parties involved.

By preparing a description written in this way, we are making it easy to draw a data flow diagram according to our advice that a level 1 DFD should have each process box corresponding to a functional area.

4.3.3 Initial attempt at current physical DFDs

In Figure 4.6 you will find a level 1 DFD. In Figures 4.7–4.9 are shown the level 2 DFDs for processes 1, 2 and 4. It has been decided not to expand process 3 (moderate and finalize results) as the description of this process is best done in another way (see Chapter 5 *Specifying processes*).

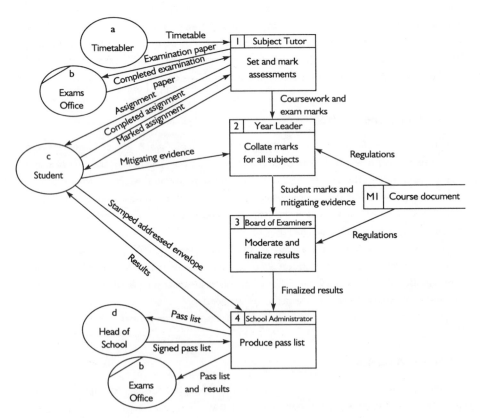

Figure 4.6   Level 1 DFD (current physical) for student assessment system

Example 2 – the student assessment system   55

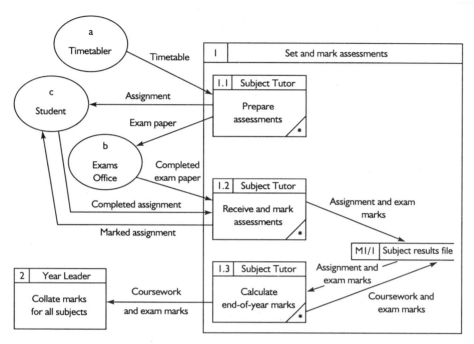

Figure 4.7 Level 2 DFD (current physical) for student assessment system process 1: Set and mark assessments

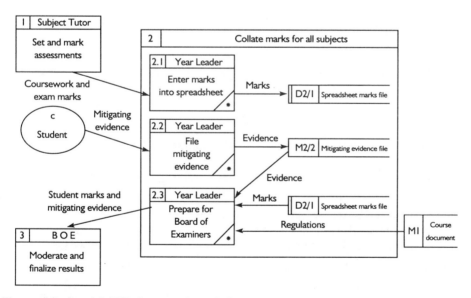

Figure 4.8 Level 2 DFD (current physical) for student assessment system process 2: Collate marks for all subjects

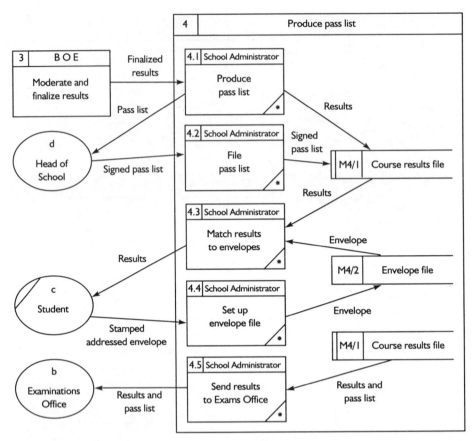

Figure 4.9   Level 2 DFD (current physical) for student assessment system process 4: Produce pass list

4.4 When is a level 2 a level 1 and vice versa?

Let us go back to the Marine Construction example for a moment. Imagine that we were only interested in the functions of the Production Office and not really bothered about the Sales, Design and Materials Offices. In this case, the level 2 DFD for the Production Office in our original example would become a *level 1 DFD* in our new scenario. In addition, the Materials Office and Sales Office which were *processes* in the original level 1 DFD would become *external entities* in the new way of looking at the system.

This idea of the *system boundary* is important. It depends on exactly what it is you are interested in. So, for example, the stock control system introduced in Chapter 3 could well be a level 1 process in a larger production system, even though it is presented as a complete system in itself in Chapter 3.

4.5 Time considerations

You will find that *time* is not really an important consideration in data flow diagrams – the first process *need not* always occur before the second, but it may. There are much more powerful techniques for showing time dependencies of processes, and you will meet two of these in Chapter 10. Data flow diagrams simply show what happens to data, where the data comes from and goes to and what data stores are referenced or updated along the way.

We hope that you are now gaining in confidence as far as data flow diagrams are concerned, for it is now time to discover what happens when the processes have been decomposed as far as possible, i.e. when we reach the bottom level.

Summary

This chapter began by explaining the problems with creating real DFDs for real systems and explained the idea of functional areas. It then went through two very different examples and guided you through the creation of a complete set of levelled DFDs for both scenarios. We want you to leave this chapter with a good understanding of creating a set of DFDs, but also with an appreciation that the different levels can be interchangeable if the boundary of the system expands or contracts.

Further reading

T. De Marco, *Structured Analysis and Systems Specification*, Yourden Press, Prentice Hall International, Englewood Cliffs, NJ, 1979. This is one of the seminal works in structured analysis and still contains one of the best descriptions of the reasons behind data flow diagramming despite the age of the book. The book is written in a very friendly style and we would recommend you having a browse as it is very inspiring.

5

Specifying processes

5.1 Introduction

5.1.1 Reaching the bottom level

DFDs are a very powerful way of describing processes, but they cannot completely describe the way things are done. When we reach the bottom level of a DFD we still need to write about what exactly it is that goes on in this bottom level. Often decisions are made or operations repeated, and to describe this we need a way of writing accurately, unambiguously and completely. These process descriptions are contained in elementary process descriptions (EPDs), and this chapter will show you some ways of writing these.

5.1.2 Accurate, unambiguous, precise and complete

The sort of language required in systems analysis descriptions is very different from everyday English, in fact different from the style of language we are using in this book. You may have noticed that we repeat ourselves quite a lot – we have mentioned logicalization several times for example and yet not explained what it involves. We are doing this because repetition is an acknowledged educational tool – remember at school when you did several mathematics examples which were all basically the same. Repetition reinforces things. We are trying to get you to realize that logicalization is really important by repeating it a lot. If you repeat yourself when you are describing a system, you are wasting time and effort, and may well end up with inefficiencies. System descriptions should be *precise and accurate*.

Have you ever watched a skilled politician talking on the television? You may believe that they have been told never to answer a question directly. Often their answers can be interpreted in a number of ways: they are ambiguous. They do this deliberately so they can appeal to a range of voters and adapt their stance to events outside of their control. Also, it is often what they *do not* say that is more interesting than what they do say. They conveniently miss things out: their answers are incomplete. Ambiguity and incompleteness in system descriptions are *potentially disastrous*. You cannot have a computer system that does not know what to do or cannot make up its mind. System descriptions need to be *accurate, unambiguous, precise and complete*.

There are a number of techniques which are used in systems analysis to capture procedures precisely. Just remember that they are geared to precision and as a result would appear very turgid and unsophisticated to an everyday reader. They are not meant to be like conversational language.

5.2 The problem with ordinary English

Let us start with an example.

A product is passed as fit for sale if it passes a mechanical test and an electrical test and has the correct dimensions. If it fails the mechanical test or the electrical test (but not both), it is sent back to the workshop for repair. In all other cases, the product is rejected.

At first sight, this may seem a fair and realistic description of a quality control process. However, it is inaccurate, and if followed exactly could lead to products being passed as fit for sale when, in reality, they should not. According to a literal interpretation of the policy, a product which has incorrect dimensions and has failed the electrical test would be sent back to the workshop for repair simply because it passed the mechanical test.

The writer means to say that a product must have the correct dimensions even to be considered as fit for sale. Because 'and has the correct dimensions' is the end of the first sentence, the writer has subconsciously assumed that this condition carries across to the start of the second sentence. The description can be written more accurately as follows.

A product is passed as fit for sale if it passes a mechanical test and an electrical test and has the correct dimensions. If it has the correct dimensions and fails the mechanical test or the electrical test (but not both), it is sent back to the workshop for repair. In all other cases, the product is rejected.

Although this description is more accurate, it suffers from being long-winded and cumbersome, and considerable concentration is required on the part of the reader. The difficulty with ordinary English is that inconsistencies and inaccuracies are easily hidden in the words, and creating an unambiguous and accurate description can lead to lengthy narrative.

5.3 Structured English

5.3.1 What it is

There is no hard and fast definition of structured English. It varies in style between its users and it varies in formality depending on the target audience. It is basically an attempt to remove the background *noise words* from narrative descriptions. It strips the description down to its bare essentials and removes ambiguity, redundancy and inconsistencies.

All forms of structured English are based on the logical constructs of

- sequence;
- selection;
- iteration.

5.3.2 Sequence

A sequence construct is simply a list of one or more actions or events and is represented by one or more imperative statements. For example:

```
Multiply Price by Quantity-Sold giving Net-Price
Multiply Net-Price by 0.175 giving VAT
Add VAT to Net-Price giving Gross-Price
```

All the actions are performed in the order given and they are all written in line. To illustrate the variations in style and syntax that abound, another way of writing the same sequence may well be:

```
Calculate Net-Price = Price * Quantity-Sold
Calculate VAT = Net-Price * 0.175
Calculate Gross-Price = Net-Price + VAT
```

5.3.3 Selection

A selection construct (sometimes called a decision construct) occurs when there are a number of alternative policies which can apply depending upon the result of some condition and only one policy is selected.

Again, different forms of structured English have different ways of implementing this, but nearly all include the IF...ELSE statements. Some terminate this with an ENDIF i.e. IF...ELSE...ENDIF. Examples are below:

```
IF dimensions not OK
   Reject product
ELSE (dimensions OK)
   IF mechanical test OK
     IF electrical test OK
       Pass product
     ELSE (electrical test not OK)
       Repair product
   ELSE (mechanical test not OK)
     IF electrical test OK
       Repair product
     ELSE (electrical test not OK)
       Reject product
```

Note the indentation and use of brackets which aids the reading and understanding of the description. An even more formal variation of writing this is below.

```
IF dimensions not OK
   Reject product
ELSE
   IF mechanical test OK
     IF electrical test OK
       Pass product
     ELSE
       Repair product
     ENDIF
   ELSE
     IF electrical test OK
       Repair product
     ELSE
       Reject product
     ENDIF
   ENDIF
ENDIF
```

The above is getting pretty close to the program code found in some programming languages. Multiple selections are sometimes implemented using the CASE construct. An example of this is as follows.

```
Select CASE
  CASE 1 (0 <= Net-Price < 100)
    Set Discount to 0
  CASE 2 (100 <= Net-Price < 200)
    Set Discount to 10%
  CASE 3 (200 <= Net-Price < 300)
    Set Discount to 15%
  CASE 4 (300 <= Net-Price < 500)
    Set Discount to 20%
  CASE 5 (Net-Price >= 500)
    Set Discount to 25%
```

5.3.4 Iteration

An iteration construct (sometimes called a repetition construct) occurs when an action or series of actions is repeated subject to a condition that governs the continued repetition. It is implemented by such formats as REPEAT...UNTIL:

```
REPEAT
  Add Invoice-Total to Overall-Total
  Add 1 to No-invoices
UNTIL no more invoices
Divide Overall-Total by No-invoices giving Average-Value
```

or WHILE...ENDWHILE:

```
WHILE more invoices
  Add Invoice-Total to Overall-Total
  Add 1 to No-invoices
ENDWHILE
Divide Overall-Total by No-invoices giving Average-Value
```

or for less formal forms of structured English by FOR ALL or FOR EACH:

```
FOR each invoice
  Add Invoice-Total to Overall-Total
  Add 1 to No-invoices
Divide Overall-Total by No-invoices giving Average-Value
```

5.3.5 Variations on structured English

Codelike structured English, which was outlined in the previous sections, may well be easy for an experienced analyst or programmer to understand as it is close to program code. There are even more formal variations such as pseudo-code which address such aspects as initialization and termination, file handling, use of flags etc.

However, to a normal user, the structured English met so far may simply be too much. One of the main aims of systems analysis is to involve users as much as possible and presenting them with rigid, formalized processing logic may very well put them off.

It is in this area that a return to a more narrative or report-like style may be appropriate, but it should still be in a concise unambiguous form. In many cases, it may be necessary to convert the description into structured English first and use this as the basis for a more accessible form of presentation. It should be possible to express a structured process description in a narrative or report-like style without the loss of logical precision, but it is not easy. As most users will be familiar with the more formal presentation found in reports, this approach is often successful.

The example of the quality control policy description could be written:

1. If a product does not have the correct dimensions reject the product.
2. If a product does have the correct dimensions, consider the mechanical and electrical tests as follows:
   (a) both tests satisfactory – pass product;
   (b) both mechanical and electrical tests unsatisfactory – reject product;
   (c) either mechanical or electrical tests unsatisfactory (but not both) – repair product.

The above description, although perhaps a little verbose and long-winded, is accurate and in a form with which most ordinary users can identify. Note that the description is equivalent to structured English and uses some of its concepts (such as indentation).

5.4 Decision tables

5.4.1 What they are

Decision tables are useful when a combination of decisions have to be made in order to establish a result. They have been around for a long time and are still widely used. They are not peculiar to computer-related areas and variations upon them occur widely in the real world. Such tables are made up of four quadrants as illustrated in Figure 5.1.

Condition stub	Condition entry
Action stub	Action entry

Figure 5.1   Decision table quadrants

There are a number of types of decision table:

- limited entry;
- extended entry;
- mixed entry.

5.4.2 Limited entry decision tables

Conditions are entered into the table as direct questions to which the answer can only be yes (Y) or no (N). All the possible combinations of Ys and Ns are placed in the condition entry quadrant of the table and each vertical set of Ys and Ns is called a rule. The possible results or actions are placed in the action stub and the relevant action(s) resulting from each rule are marked in the action entry quadrant with an 'X'.

Let us examine the product quality control problem. First, identify the *conditions*. These are:

Correct dimensions?

Passed mechanical test?

Passed electrical test?

Note that it is important not to include mutually exclusive conditions such as *Failed mechanical test?* as this is catered for by a 'N' answer to *Passed mechanical test?*

Next identify the actions. These are:

accept product;

repair product;

reject product.

Finally determine the *number of rules* using the formula 2^N where N is the number of conditions. Hence, in this case, there are $2^3 = 8$ rules.

The decision table can now be constructed as in Figure 5.2. Note how the Ys and Ns are laid out in a set pattern to ensure that all combinations are catered for.

Correct dimensions?	Y	Y	Y	Y	N	N	N	N
Passed mechanical test?	Y	Y	N	N	Y	Y	N	N
Passed electrical test?	Y	N	Y	N	Y	N	Y	N
Accept product	X							
Repair product		X	X					
Reject product				X	X	X	X	X

Figure 5.2   Product quality control decision table – version 1

Examination of the table shows that redundancy exists. If the answer to the first question is N, the answers to the second and third questions are irrelevant. Redundancy occurs when two or more rules lead to the same action. It may be feasible to eliminate unnecessary conditions by inserting a '–' entry in appropriate places as in Figure 5.3.

Correct dimensions?	Y	Y	Y	Y	N
Passed mechanical test?	Y	Y	N	N	–
Passed electrical test?	Y	N	Y	N	–
Accept product	X				
Repair product		X	X		
Reject product				X	X

Figure 5.3   Product quality control decision table – version 2

The ELSE rule can be used to simplify a table even further as in Figure 5.4.

Correct dimensions?	Y	Y	Y	E
Passed mechanical test?	Y	Y	N	L
Passed electrical test?	Y	N	Y	S
				E
Accept product	X			
Repair product		X	X	
Reject product				X

Figure 5.4   Product quality control decision table – version 3

5.4.3 Extended entry decision tables

Where the conditions are all inter-related to each other, limited entry decision tables can be very unwieldy. For example, the table in Figure 5.5 shows the alphabetical grades associated with percentage marks awarded in an assessment. By limiting the

Mark 0–34?	Y	N	N	N	N	N
Mark 35–39?	–	Y	N	N	N	N
Mark 40–49?	–	–	Y	N	N	N
Mark 50–59?	–	–	–	Y	N	N
Mark 60–69?	–	–	–	–	Y	N
Mark >69?	–	–	–	–	–	Y
Grade F	X					
Grade E		X				
Grade D			X			
Grade C				X		
Grade B					X	
Grade A						X

Figure 5.5   Assessment policy decision table – limited entry

kinds of entry we have created an over-complicated view of the situation. An *extended entry* decision table replaces the condition entries of Y and N and the action entries of Xs with actual values as in Figure 5.6.

Mark	0–34	35–39	40–49	50–59	60–69	>69
Grade	F	E	D	C	B	A

Figure 5.6 Assessment policy decision table – extended entry

5.4.4 Mixed entry decision tables

Both limited and extended entry lines may be used in the same table, but a mixture cannot occur within a single line, for example in Figure 5.7.

Regular customer?	Y	Y	Y	N	N	N
Order value £	0–99	100–500	>500	0–99	100–500	>500
Discount given	0	15%	20%	0	10%	15%
Free gift			X			X

Figure 5.7 Sales policy decision table – mixed entry

5.5 Decision trees

We have already seen how useful tree diagrams can be, in Chapter 2. We now come to their most common use within the recognized systems analysis techniques, as an alternative to a decision table. They tend to be easier to understand because they are virtually self-explanatory. For example, the employment policy problem is shown in Figure 5.8.

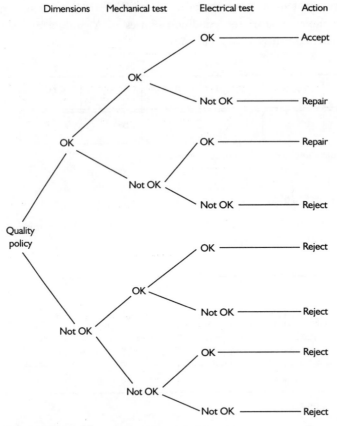

Figure 5.8   Product quality control decision tree

5.6 A worked example – the end-of-year assessment system ▬ ●

5.6.1 Background

We will now demonstrate the application of what has gone before, by considering an example which concerns the end-of-year assessment of students on the second year of a four year degree course in business computing. The procedures describe the processing involved in processes 2.3 and 3 of the student assessment system introduced in Chapter 4.

Students study six subjects:

quantitative methods;

systems analysis and design;

computer systems;

programming;

business studies;

behavioural studies.

Students are assessed in each subject by coursework and an end-of-year examination. For all subjects except programming, the coursework counts for 20% and the examination 80% of the final subject mark. In programming, the coursework counts for 40% and the examination 60%.

After the examinations, the Year Leader receives from each Subject Tutor a list of all coursework and examination marks. A document must be prepared for the Board of Examiners showing for each student coursework marks, examination marks and overall subject marks for each subject. This document should also highlight any failed marks. The rules for determining failure are as follows:

A student has failed a subject if:

- the coursework mark is below 40%; or
- the examination mark is below 35%, or
- the subject mark is below 40%.

Note that it is possible for a student to pass the coursework and the examination, but to still fail the subject. The Board of Examiners has certain guidelines which are used to decide the fate of students. The Board does, however, have the power to condone marks if the student has justifiable reasons for not doing well (such as medical problems etc.). However, we shall concentrate on the formal rules which apply and ignore any exceptional circumstances.

If students fail three or more subjects they are allowed to repeat the year unless they already are repeat students, in which case they are required to leave the course. A repeat is either internal or external. If any of the subjects failed include a failure in coursework or in the overall subject mark, the student can only repeat internally, i.e. they have to resit the year on a full-time basis. If the subjects failed are entirely due to poor performance in the examinations and all the coursework marks and overall subject marks are satisfactory, the student is given the choice of repeating internally or externally. External repeats are only required to resit the examinations in the following year.

If students fail one or two subjects, they are allowed to be reassessed in those subjects before the start of the next academic year. If students fail on coursework, they are given extra coursework. If they fail an examination they must resit it. If they fail the overall subject mark, they have to resit the exam and do extra coursework, regardless of the marks obtained in each element. The subsequent results of these students are considered at a later Board of Examiners, but the procedures involved will not be discussed.

5.6.2 Representing the narrative description

The above description is quite long-winded and probably contains some omissions, inconsistencies and ambiguities. However, it is meant to contain enough information to enable a reasonable understanding of the procedures employed. The procedures are represented (Figure 5.9) as a fragment of the data flow diagram first seen in Chapter 4.

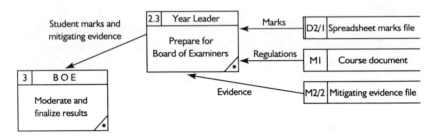

Figure 5.9   Fragment of level 1 DFD for student assessment system (from Figure 4.8)

We will now take each process in turn, and see how they may be described. To begin with, we describe process 2.3 in two ways – first in a fairly formal style of structured English (Figure 5.10), and then in a more *user-friendly* manner (Figure 5.11).

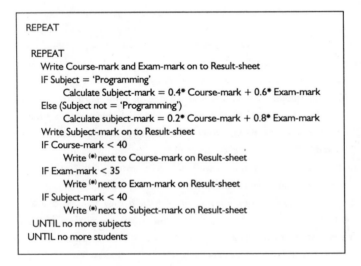

```
REPEAT

   REPEAT
      Write Course-mark and Exam-mark on to Result-sheet
      IF Subject = 'Programming'
         Calculate Subject-mark = 0.4* Course-mark + 0.6* Exam-mark
      Else (Subject not = 'Programming')
         Calculate subject-mark = 0.2* Course-mark + 0.8* Exam-mark
      Write Subject-mark on to Result-sheet
      IF Course-mark < 40
         Write (*) next to Course-mark on Result-sheet
      IF Exam-mark < 35
         Write (*) next to Exam-mark on Result-sheet
      IF Subject-mark < 40
         Write (*) next to Subject-mark on Result-sheet
   UNTIL no more subjects
UNTIL no more students
```

Figure 5.10   Process 2.3 Prepare for Board of Examiners (formal style)

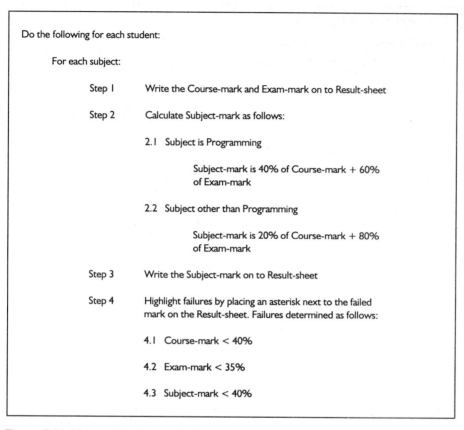

Do the following for each student:

    For each subject:

        Step 1   Write the Course-mark and Exam-mark on to Result-sheet

        Step 2   Calculate Subject-mark as follows:

                2.1 Subject is Programming

                        Subject-mark is 40% of Course-mark + 60% of Exam-mark

                2.2 Subject other than Programming

                        Subject-mark is 20% of Course-mark + 80% of Exam-mark

        Step 3   Write the Subject-mark on to Result-sheet

        Step 4   Highlight failures by placing an asterisk next to the failed mark on the Result-sheet. Failures determined as follows:

                4.1 Course-mark < 40%

                4.2 Exam-mark < 35%

                4.3 Subject-mark < 40%

Figure 5.11   Process 2.3 Prepare for Board of Examiners (user friendly style)

Process 3 is more involved than process 2.3. The way in which it is described in Figure 5.12 combines basic constructs of structured English with decision tables.

This example based upon process 3 illustrates the hybrid nature of some structured descriptions, i.e. using an appropriate mixture of ways to give the best description. At all times, the target audience must be borne in mind. This is the single most important factor in determining the style used in specifying processes.

Do the following for each student:

Step 1 Determine the number of failed subjects:

      A subject is failed if any of the following are asterisked:
        – Course-mark
        – Exam-mark
        – Subject-mark

Step 2 Determine student results:

      CASE 1 (Number of subjects failed = 0)
        Student has passed the year
      CASE 2 (Number of subjects failed = 1 or 2)
        For each subject determine the result according to the following decision table:

Course-mark < 40%	Y	N	N	E
Exam-mark < 35%	N	Y	N	L
Subject-mark < 40%	N	N	N	S
				E
Redo coursework	X			X
Resit exam		X		X
Subject passed			X	

CASE 3 (Number of subjects failed > 2)
      Determine result according to the following decision table:

Repeat student?	Y	N	N	N
Any Course-mark < 40%	–	Y	N	N
Any Subject-mark < 40%	–	–	Y	N
Leave course	X			
Internal repeat		X	X	
Internal or external repeat				X

Figure 5.12 Process 3 Moderate and finalize results

We trust that by this stage you really feel as though you are getting somewhere with DFDs and the processes which they contain. Our aim has been to give you a good fundamental understanding of their usefulness and how to create them. We are going to leave DFDs for the present, but we return to them in Chapter 8 where we discover what they have to offer in terms of working out the logical happenings within a physical system, and how important this is to the systems design objective.

For the next two chapters we stop concentrating on what makes the data *flow*, i.e. the activities that take place within a system and drive the data around it. Instead, we turn our attention to the data itself – its organization and its structure. We show how the systems analyst answers questions such as what data stores (or files) a system needs, what data each should contain, and the relationships which need to exist within and between these data stores.

Summary

This chapter began by explaining the problems with specifying processes and then introduced you to structured English. It went on to the various types of decision tables and decision trees. It finished with a couple of fairly complicated examples illustrating the hybrid nature of many structured process specifications.

Further reading

S. Skidmore, *Introducing Systems Analysis*, Chapter 7, NCC Blackwell, Oxford, 1994.

6

Data modelling

6.1 Processes and data

In systems analysis it is necessary to view a system not only either physically or logically as explained earlier (Chapter 2), but also in terms of either processing or data. Processes are the activities which are performed in the system and are described by data flow diagrams, decision tables and structured English. By data, we mean data stored within the system that is needed by the system in order for it to function. Data is often used by processes in a variety of ways. Processes can add to data, remove it, change it (or update it) or simply refer to it. In efficient systems, data is always *organized*. So in a sales order processing system there are likely to be customer details stored together in a *Customer File*, product details in a *Product File* and so on. These files will themselves be organised into some sort of *order*. Each customer may well be allocated a customer number and the file will probably be organised in customer number sequence to help in searching. The different files are often linked or cross-referenced. For example, a customer may well order a particular product on a regular basis and this fact needs to be stored somewhere in the system.

This chapter looks at ways of identifying things which need to be stored in a system and the relationships between these things. We will start with some basic concepts.

6.2 Entities and attributes

6.2.1 Entities

The most important concept in data modelling is that of an entity.

An entity is a thing of interest to a system about which data is kept.

In computer systems, an entity is normally equivalent to a file. For example, in a hospital administration system, some likely entities are: Patient, Doctor, Operation and Ward. Each of these things are is interest to the system and will have data stored about it. Look at the following list and decide which you think are likely candidates for entities. Think about whether it is likely that data will stored about each of them.

1. A member of staff in a personnel system.
2. A book in a library system.
3. A customer's address in a sales system.
4. A customer in a sales system.
5. A National Insurance number in a payroll system.
6. A patient in a medical records system.
7. The library in a library system.

The only entities in the above list are (1), (2), (4) and (6). Each of these is likely to have data stored about it. Some likely data items for each of these are:

1. Name, address, date of birth.
2. Book title, author, publisher.
4. Name, address, credit limit.
6. National Insurance number, date of birth.

Option (3) is not an entity. A customer's address is data *about a customer* and so is an attribute (see later), not an entity.

In the same way, option (5) is not an entity as National Insurance number is an attribute of an employee in a payroll system.

Option (7) is tricky. A thing is only an entity if it is possible for there to be more than one occurrence of it in the system. As there is only one library in say, a school's library system, it is not an entity. However, if there were several libraries, such as in a local authority or some universities, then the library would be an entity.

6.2.2 Attributes

You have just been introduced to the term attribute. It is now time to define it.

An attribute is an item of data held about an entity. It is equivalent to a data item.

In computer systems, an attribute is equivalent to a field on a record. A record is equivalent to an entity occurrence.

A special and very important type of attribute is the key attribute.

A key attribute uniquely identifies a specific occurrence of an entity.

For example, in a sales system, customer name and address are attributes of the entity customer. The key attribute is likely to be Customer Code or Customer Number which is unique to each customer.

See if you can choose likely key and non-key attributes for the following entities:

1. A car in a vehicle registration system.
2. An employee in a payroll system.
3. An item of stock in a stock control system.

For (1), the key is likely to be the car's registration number, with non-key attributes such as car make, car model, date of manufacture etc. For (2), the key is likely to be employee number or payroll number with non-key attributes such as name, address, department, tax code etc. For (3), the key is likely to be a stock number (or part number) with non-key attributes such as description, amount in stock, price etc.

6.2.3 Selecting entities

Deciding upon entities is not always as easy as you might think. Sometimes, entities turn out to be really attributes and vice versa. A good place to start is to look at all the *nouns* in a description of a system and think deeply about whether data is likely to be stored about them or not. You may like to have a go at the following description. Start by selecting all the nouns and think about whether each noun is a likely entity or attribute or neither. The description is a very simplified account of a vehicle breakdown and rescue service, which employs engineers to help its members when they have trouble with their vehicles.

Each engineer is allocated one van (which is driven up to a certain mileage and then replaced). Each member has only one address but perhaps many vehicles. Each visit is to deal with only one vehicle. A member can be visited more than once on any given date, and there may be many visits to a member on different dates. A member may only be covered for some of the vehicles they own and not for others.

The nouns in the description are: *engineer, van, mileage, member, address, vehicle, visit* and *date*. The likely entities are:

engineer – possible attributes include name, address and telephone number;

van – possible attributes include registration number and mileage;

member – possible attributes include membership number, name, address and telephone number;

vehicle – possible attributes include registration number, make and model;

visit – possible attributes include date of visit, purpose of visit and cost of visit.

For the other nouns in the description:

mileage is likely to be an attribute of the entity *van*;

address is likely to be an attribute of the entity *customer*;

date is likely to be an attribute of the entity *visit*.

6.3 Entity relationships

6.3.1 Identifying relationships

What makes data modelling such a powerful and interesting subject is the fact that entities are *related* to one another. Let us look at some of the entities in a particular sales order processing system that supplies and fits kitchens.

A sale always starts with a customer receiving an estimate. The estimate then becomes an order. An order can be for one or more stock items. Each stock item belongs to a certain stock category (e.g. taps, sinks, cupboards etc.).

We will leave it at that even though there is obviously a lot more to the system such as invoices, payments etc. By looking at the nouns in the description and using some common sense, we can arrive at the list of likely entities in Figure 6.1 together with their key and some non-key attributes.

In a personnel system, an Employee is related to a Department because an Employee belongs to a Department and a Department contains a number of Employees. You would expect this system to be able to tell you which Department a particular

Entity	Key attribute	Some non-key attributes
Estimate	Estimate Number or Order Number	Date Customer Code Stock Item Codes
Order	Order Number	Same as Estimate
Customer	Customer Code	Customer Name Customer Address Credit Limit
Stock Item	Stock Item Code	Description Number in Stock Supplier Code
Stock Category	Category Code	Category Description

Figure 6.1   Entities with their key and non-key attributes

Employee works in and which Employees are in a particular Department. In our kitchen supply system, we would probably have several relationships between entities. In Figure 6.2 an X has been used to indicate a relationship between two entities.

Because the relationships are shown in a grid, each one appears twice. So an X is placed in both places where Estimate and Order intersect. Why are these entities related? The relationships are written out below:

an Estimate becomes an Order;

an Estimate is issued to a particular Customer;

an Estimate refers to Stock Item(s);

an Order is placed by a Customer;

an Order refers to Stock Item(s);

a Stock Item belongs to a particular Stock Category.

	Estimate	Order	Customer	Stock Item	Stock Category
Estimate		X	X	X	
Order	X		X	X	
Customer	X	X			
Stock Item	X	X			X
Stock Category				X	

Figure 6.2 Relationships between entities

Please bear in mind that this is all a little loose and is really intended to get you to understand the general idea. The above relationships are still *one-way*. It is more complete to say that an Estimate becomes an Order *and* an Order is derived from an Estimate. This makes the relationship *two-way*. Also, you may well think that a Customer is related to a Stock Item because a customer orders stock items; however, they are linked via the entity Order. It should become clearer as we explore the topic further. The chapter on relational data analysis really sorts out any problems we may still have with which entities are linked.

6.3.2 Degrees of relationship

There is more to this than meets the eye. It is not enough to say that two entities are related. We need to say to what degree they are related. For example, can a Customer only place *one and only one* Order, and can an Order be placed by *one and only one* Customer? the answer to the first part is *no* and the answer to the second part is *yes*. A Customer can place several Orders if they so wish, but one Order can only be placed by one Customer. Each of the relationships can be analysed in this way giving the following relationship statements.

1. A Customer can be issued with *one or more* Estimates and an Estimate is issued to *only one* Customer. This is known as a one-to-many relationship, and is drawn as shown in Figure 6.3. The *crow's foot* goes at the *many* end of the relationship. It is usual to show the *many* end beneath the *one* end. This type of relationship is often called the master–detail relationship and the master should go on top.

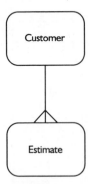

Figure 6.3 The one-to-many relationship between Customer and Estimate

2. A Customer can place *one or more* Orders and an Order is placed by *only one* Customer. This is another one-to-many relationship, as shown in Figure 6.4.

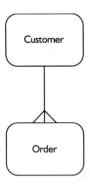

Figure 6.4 The one-to-many relationship between Customer and Order

3. An Estimate can become *only one* Order and an Order is derived from *only one* Estimate. This is known as a one-to-one relationship and is shown in Figure 6.5. Because both sides of the relationship have the same degree, it is normal to draw it horizontally.

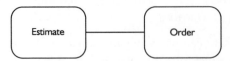

Figure 6.5 The one-to-one relationship between Estimate and Order

4. An Estimate refers to *one or more* Stock Items and a Stock Item may be present on *one or more* Estimates. This is known as a many-to-many relationship and is

shown in Figure 6.6. In this figure there are two *crow's feet* as the relationship is many-to-many. Again, this is drawn horizontally like the one-to-one relationship.

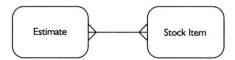

Figure 6.6   The many-to-many relationship between Estimate and Stock Item

5. An Order refers to *one or more* Stock Items and a Stock Item may be present on *one or more* Orders. This is the same as the last one – a many-to-many relationship. See Figure 6.7.

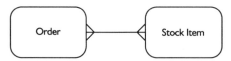

Figure 6.7   The many-to-many relationship between Order and Stock Item

6. A Stock Item will belong to *only one* Stock Category and a Stock Category will contain *one or more* Stock Items. This is a one-to-many relationship again (see Figure 6.8).

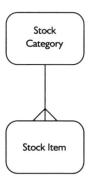

Figure 6.8   The one-to-many relationship between Stock Category and Stock Item

6.3.3 Optionality

Some relationships are *mandatory* and some are *optional*. For example, in our sales system, some Customers may be on file even if they do not have a current Estimate or Order (i.e. regular or account Customers). However, an Estimate cannot exist without a Customer. The complete relationship is shown in Figure 6.9. The dotted line indicates that this part of the relationship is *optional*. The full line indicates that this part of the relationship is *mandatory* (or compulsory).

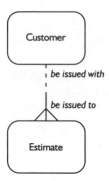

Figure 6.9 The one-to-many relationship between Customer and Estimate, showing optionality

The relationship should be read as follows: One Customer *may* be issued with *one or more* Estimates and one Estimate *must* be issued to *only one* Customer. It is normal to write the description of the relationship against the line joining the two entities.

The rest of the relationships for the sales system can now be drawn and written.

1. One Customer *may* place *one or more* Orders and one Order *must* be placed by *only one* Customer (Figure 6.10).

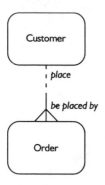

Figure 6.10 The one-to-many relationship between Customer and Order, showing optionality

2. One Estimate *may* become *only one* Order and one Order *must* be derived from *only one* Estimate (Figure 6.11).

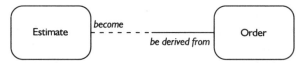

Figure 6.11   The one-to-one relationship between Estimate and Order, showing optionality

3. One Estimate *must* refer to *one or more* Stock Items and one Stock Item *may* be present on *one or more* Estimates (Figure 6.12).

Figure 6.12   The many-to-many relationship between Estimate and Stock Item, showing optionality

4. One Order *must* refer to *one or more* Stock Items and one Stock Item *may* be present on *one or more* Orders (Figure 6.13).

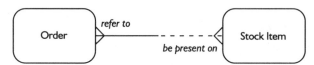

Figure 6.13   The many-to-many relationship between Order and Stock Item, showing optionality

5. One Stock Item *must* belong to *only one* Stock Category and one Stock Category *must* contain *one or more* Stock Items (Figure 6.14).

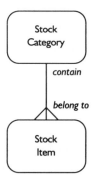

Figure 6.14   The one-to-many relationship between Stock Category and Stock Item, showing optionality

6.3.4 Entities and entity occurrences

We often find that some students get a little mixed up at this stage. Look back at Figure 6.10, the one-to-many relationship between Customer and Order. When told that one Order *must* be placed by *only one* Customer, we sometimes hear the comment 'Surely there is more than one customer'. Of course there are several Customers in the system. Each particular Customer is an *entity occurrence* of the *entity* Customer. The entity Customer is, if you like, the *idea* or *map* of a Customer and describes the data items stored for the Customer. The details of the actual occurrences of Customer then map onto these data items with real values.

So, even though there are several Customers in the system giving several occurrences of the entity Customer, it still remains true that one occurrence of an Order can only be placed by one occurrence of a Customer.

6.3.5 Further examples

Try the following four exercises. The entities are in capital letters. Connect the entities together with relationships. Show optionality and describe the relationship against the lines. Check your answers with the solutions given in Figure 6.15.

1. An EMPLOYEE may be a MEMBER of the company's sports club which is exclusive to the company's employees.
2. A ROOM may have a number of telephone EXTENSIONS but may not have any. A telephone EXTENSION must belong to a ROOM.
3. A COURSE must have a number of STUDENTS enrolled on it and a STUDENT must be enrolled on only one COURSE.
4. A STUDENT must be enrolled on only one COURSE and a COURSE must have STUDENTS enrolled on it. Each COURSE must have a number of MODULES and a MODULE can be part of more than one COURSE but must be part of at least one COURSE. Each MODULE must have a LECTURER as subject leader but a LECTURER may not necessarily be a subject leader or may lead more than one MODULE.

6.3.6 Many-to-many relationships

When a system is first investigated, it is often the case that many-to-many relationships appear to be present. We have already seen some in this chapter. However, these relationships *always* imply a missing or *link* entity. An example will illustrate this point.

In a doctors' practice where there are a number of doctors, a doctor can have

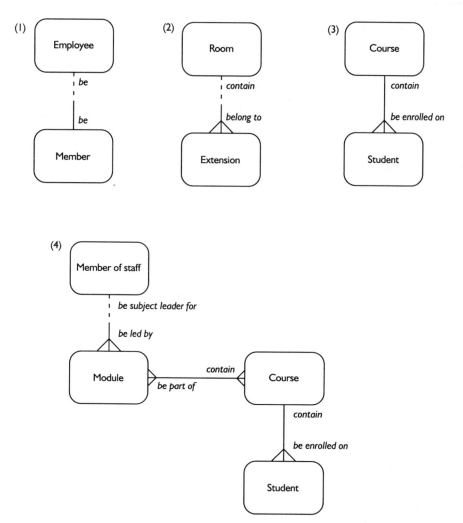

Figure 6.15   Solutions to exercises in Section 6.3.5

appointments with a number of patients and a patient can have appointments with more than one doctor (even.though they generally have one regular doctor). At first sight this seems a candidate for a many-to-many relationship.

One Doctor *may* have an appointment with *one or more* Patients and one Patient *may* have an appointment with *one or more* Doctors (see Figure 6.16).

Note that both sides of this relationship are *optional* which may surprise you. It is possible for a doctor's details to be stored in the system before they have had any appointments and similarly for a patient. It is simply a question of time, and this

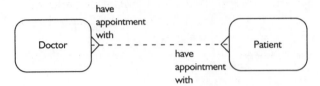

Figure 6.16   Many-to-many relationship between Doctor and Patient

time factor often introduces optionality into a relationship which at first sight would appear to be mandatory.

There is a *missing* entity – hidden in the relationship description. You must ask the question: 'Is there an entity in the system to cope with the situation where there is *only one* Doctor and *only one* Patient?'. The answer is obviously Appointment and this is the missing link entity. The many-to-many relationship is then *resolved* as in Figure 6.17.

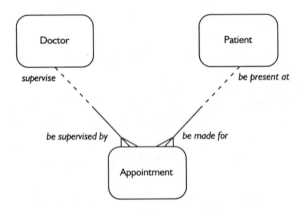

Figure 6.17   Resolution of many-to-many relationship between Doctor and Patient

A many-to-many relationship is always resolved in this way, with each of the original entities forming a one-to-many relationship with the link entity. Remember the many-to-many relationship between Order and Stock Item we met earlier in the chapter? – see Figure 6.18. To resolve this, we have to think about the thing where

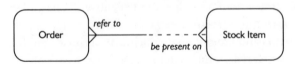

Figure 6.18   Many-to-many relationship between Order and Stock Item

one Order and one Stock Item meet. This is the individual lines of the order called Order Line. The resolved relationship is as shown in Figure 6.19. If you look at the ways in which Figure 6.16 was transformed into Figure 6.17 and Figure 6.18 into Figure 6.19, it is not too difficult to see a set of rules emerging for the resolution of many-to-many links.

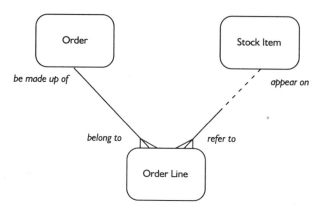

Figure 6.19 Resolution of many-to-many relationship between Order and Stock Item

Rule 1. A many-to-many link *must always* be resolved by creating a new link entity.

Rule 2. The link entity is joined to each original entity by a one-to-many relationship with the *many* end at the link entity.

Rule 3. The half of the relationship nearest the link entity is *always* mandatory (i.e. a solid line).

Rule 4. The other half of the relationship has the same optionality as in the original many-to-many relationship.

Rule 5. If it is difficult to name the link entity between entity A and entity B, simply call it A/B Link.

Rule 6. Finally, name the relationships.

6.3.7 Multiple relationships

In some situations, two or more different relationships can exist between a pair of entities. For example, a University Lecturer may be the sponsor for one or more student projects (i.e. they come up with the idea for the project in the first place). However, the sponsor may not supervise the project and lecturers may well supervise projects which they have not sponsored. Hence there are two different relationships between lecturer and project – see Figure 6.20.

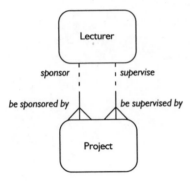

Figure 6.20   Multiple relationship between Lecturer and Project

6.3.8 Exclusive relationships

It is possible for a master entity to have detail entities which are mutually exclusive and vice versa. For example, a Customer is either issued with Invoices for each transaction or a Statement at the end of the month, never both. The relationships are exclusive: only one can exist for a particular Customer. It is drawn as shown in Figure 6.21, with the exclusivity being shown by an *exclusive arc*.

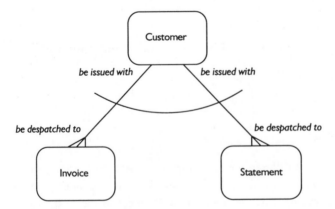

Figure 6.21   Exclusive relationships between Customer and Invoice, and Customer and Statement

6.4 Building an entity model

6.4.1 The example

We will approach this section by developing an entity model for an example system. Please note that the terms *data model* and *logical data structure* may also be used instead of the term *entity model*. They mean the same thing. The example system is described below:

A company which rents out country cottages for holidays uses a system to keep track of bookings made by customers in relation to particular cottages. Each cottage belongs to a specific owner and each owner is dealt with by a sales representative. However, not all sales representatives are allocated owners; a number of these representatives are responsible for a set of regions instead. A region is a geographic location made up of a number of areas in which the company has holiday cottages. Each cottage belongs to a particular class and each cottage will contain facilities (e.g. central heating, shower, games room etc.). The same facility may of course be available in a number of different cottages.

6.4.2 Selecting entities

Examination of the system description yields the following as likely entities:

Customer, Cottage, Booking, Owner, Sales Rep., Region, Area, Class, Facility.

6.4.3 Identifying relationships between entities

It is often useful to draw a grid with both rows and columns containing the entity names. At the intersections, we put the nature of any relationship. See Figure 6.22. As you can see, each relationship is shown twice. The row entry is the *first* entity in the relationship and the column entry the *second*. So, for example, the relationship between Area and Cottage is 1:M (one-to-many), whereas Cottage to Area is M:1 (many-to-one). M:N stands for many-to-many.

	Cus	Cot	Bking	Ownr	S Rep	Regn	Area	Cls	Fcty
Customer			I : M						
Cottage			I : M	M : I			M : I	M : I	M : N
Booking	M : I	M : I							
Owner		I : M			M : I				
Sales Rep				I : M		I : M			
Region					M : I		I : M		
Area		I : M				M : I			
Class		I : M							
Facility		M : N							

Figure 6.22   Entity relationship grid

6.4.4 Drawing the relationships

Each relationship is now drawn as shown in Figure 6.23. The diagrams include optionality and relationship names. The optionality has been derived from a combination of common sense and careful inspection of the system description.

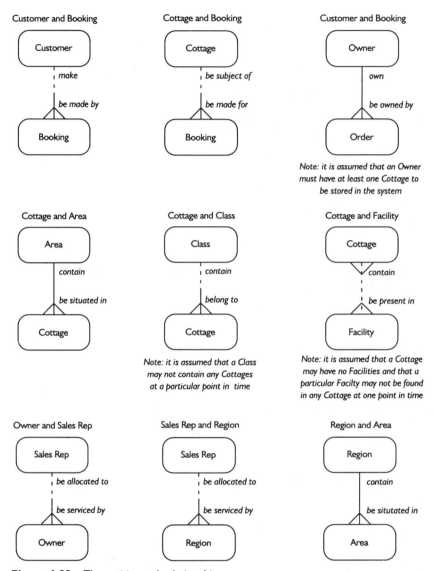

Figure 6.23   The entities and relationships

6.4.5 Completing the entity model

We are now in a position to join the whole thing together as shown in Figure 6.24. Note the introduction of the exclusive arc, and the resolution of the many-to-many relationship between Cottage and Facility.

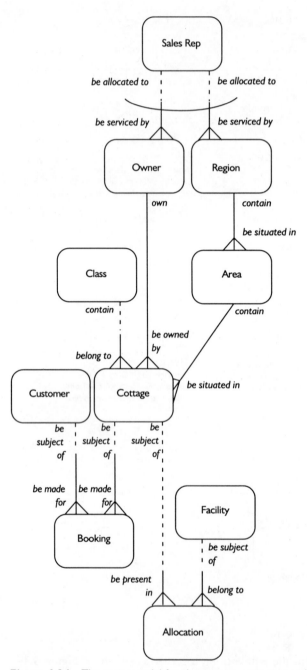

Figure 6.24   The entity model for the country cottage rental system

6.4.6 Further examples

To conclude this chapter, try these two examples and compare your answers with the solutions which follow in Figures 6.25 and 6.26. The entities are in capital letters.

Library system

> There must be at least one BOOK COPY of each BOOK TITLE in the system. Each BOOK TITLE must belong to one particular CATEGORY, but a CATEGORY can exist in the system if there are no BOOK TITLES belonging to it. LOANS are stored in the system only if they are current (i.e. when a book is returned, the record of the loan is removed). A BORROWER can have several LOANS (or none at all) and each LOAN is for one BOOK COPY.

Project management system

> A computer consultancy undertakes a number of PROJECTS. A PROJECT is for either an external CLIENT or an internal DEPARTMENT. A PROJECT must be for one or the other. A CLIENT or DEPARTMENT may have several PROJECTS on the go. Some DEPARTMENTS and CLIENTS are stored in the system even if there are no current PROJECTS for

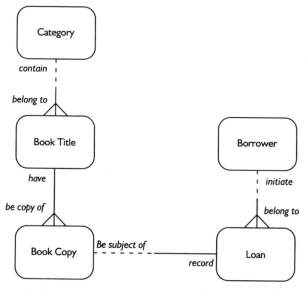

Figure 6.25 The entity model for the library system

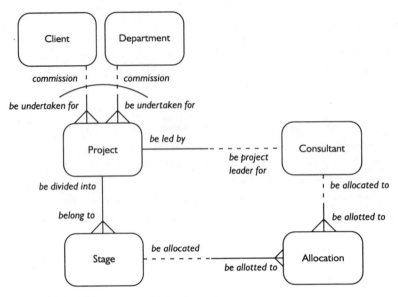

Figure 6.26   The entity model for the project management system

them. A PROJECT is split up into STAGES and there must be at least one STAGE stored in the system for each PROJECT. CONSULTANTS are allocated to each STAGE of a PROJECT. One CONSULTANT may be involved with several STAGES and each STAGE may have several CONSULTANTS. CONSULTANT details are still stored in the system even if they are not allocated to STAGES. For each PROJECT, one of the CONSULTANTS must be the project leader. A CONSULTANT is not necessarily a project leader, but they can only be project leader for one PROJECT.

Summary

This chapter began by introducing you to the concept of entities and attributes. It then looked at the different ways in which entities can be related to each other in terms of one-to-one, one-to-many and many-to-many links. The concept of optionality was introduced followed by a method of resolving a many-to-many relationship. Some special types of relationship were covered and we finished with an example of how an entity model is built. Entity modelling is a very important topic and the next chapter takes it even further, delving into the mathematically based concepts behind normalization.

Further reading

D. R. Howe, *Data Analysis for Data Base Design*, 2nd edn, Edward Arnold, London, 1989.

7

Normalization

This chapter follows on from the previous one on data modelling and is very much linked to it. If you do not yet feel comfortable with the data modelling concepts described, it may be worth reading the previous chapter again before continuing.

7.1 What is a relationship?

7.1.1 The data model

In the data modelling chapter, we finished with a data model for a system which deals with the booking of country cottages. Part of that data model is shown in Figure 7.1.

You will remember that the construction of this data model was quite methodical, but we did warn you that the whole thing was a little *loose*. Let us explain what we mean by this.

There is obviously a relationship between Cottage and Owner because an Owner owns a Cottage. Also a Customer makes a Booking and so there is an obvious relationship here. In fact, one cannot really argue with any of the relationships in the data model. However, what if someone suggested that there was a direct relationship between Customer and Owner because a Customer really makes a booking with an Owner? They would be correct that a relationship existed, but not a direct one. Customer and Owner *are* linked, but the link is *through* the two other entities Booking and Cottage.

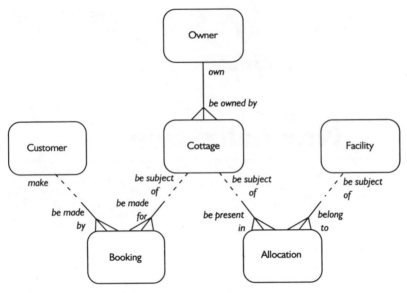

Figure 7.1   Part of the country cottage rental system

When the data model was developed in the last chapter, you were very much guided to the answer by the way the description was written, but what if it is not so obvious? There must be a more systematic (perhaps even mathematical) way of getting a correct data model than the rather subjective approach used in the last chapter.

7.1.2 Computer system relationships

In the cottage booking data model, the relationships represent the ways in which the entities interact from a system point of view. So, a Customer makes a Booking and a Booking is made for a Cottage. When we initially investigate a system, it is this sort of *business* relationship we are interested in. However, in a computer system the relationships mean something very much more precise than this. If the holiday cottage data model was stored in a computer system, it would mean that the entities were linked within the computer system. So, if the Cottage details were to hand on a computer screen or in a computer program, the system would be able to get *directly* to the Owner details for that Cottage. Similarly, it would be possible for the system to get from an Allocation to the Facility or the Cottage *directly*.

The way this is done depends upon the type of database management system used. The most common and widely used type of database is called a *relational* database (for example, ORACLE) and this is the type we will describe in this chapter. In a relational database, the Cottage and Owner would be linked by a *foreign key* as shown in Figure 7.2.

Figure 7.2   Cottage and Owner linked by foreign key

Within the Cottage entity would be stored the key of the Owner of that Cottage which is the Owner Code. This provides the link to the Owner entity for that Cottage. The Owner Code is a foreign key as it is not a key in the Cottage entity but is a key in the Owner entity. Note that the key fields are underlined and an asterisk is placed to the left of a foreign key.

In a relational database, Allocation would be linked to Facility and Cottage by a *compound* key as shown in Figure 7.3. A compound key is made up of two or more

Figure 7.3   Facility and Cottage linked through Allocation

simple keys, in this case Facility Code and Cottage Code, to provide a unique identifier for an entity. If you think about it, both Facility Code and Cottage Code are needed to identify an Allocation uniquely. Facility Code on its own is not enough as. a Facility can be present in several Cottages. It is very often the case that a compound key is the key for a *link* entity between two other entities which have a many-to-many relationship. This is the case with Allocation.

You can see the links are similar for a foreign key and a compound key. The thing which causes the link is a data item or data items. All of the links in a data model are forged in this way in a relational database, and for the fragment of the holiday cottage system it is shown in Figure 7.4.

However, how do we get to the situation where we know which entities have simple keys, which have compound keys and which contain foreign keys? The answer is by using the technique called *normalization*.

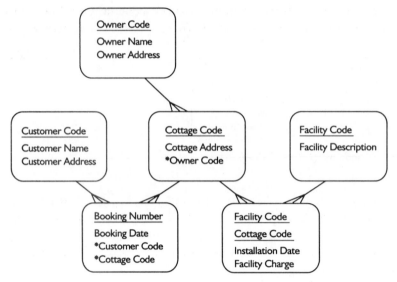

Figure 7.4   The country cottage rental system, showing use of key attributes

7.2 Normalization of documents

7.2.1 Introduction

Before we launch into this topic, we want to admit that it can be a difficult one to master. Students often struggle with it. Our reason for its inclusion is a sound one, however, and we have done our best to make it as understandable as possible. Analysts who know how to apply normalization are at a considerable advantage when it comes to drawing data structures which are reliable and complete.

We will use an approach of ours that you should be getting used to by now; i.e. by going through a couple of examples and then analysing exactly what it is we have done. Both are taken from a student records system, which is present in some shape or form in most universities. The university in the examples operates a modular system in which students study modules and gain credits for these modules until they have enough credits to qualify for a degree. The exact nature of these modules depends upon the course on which the student is enrolled, but generally speaking a particular module can be part of more than one course.

7.2.2 The student transcript

The document

One of the outputs from this system is a *student transcript* document which details the modules undertaken so far by each student and the results obtained, and this forms the basis for the first example; see Figure 7.5.

Student Number: 1078654X
Student Name: David Green
Course Code: G105
Course Title: BA Business Computing

Module Code	Module Title	Number of Credits	Grade Point	Result Code	Result
BUS119	Business Operations	20	10	P	Pass
COM110	Introduction to Computing	20	8	P	Pass
COM112	Application Building	20	3	RE	Refer exam
COM114	Software Engineering	20	2	DC	Defer coursework
COM118	Computer Law	10	9	P	Pass
COM120	Systems Analysis	20	3	RCE	Refer coursework and exam
COM122	HCI	10	7	P	Pass

Figure 7.5 The student transcript document

This document is to be output from a system, and so the data contained in the document must be stored in the system. Before we analyse this document properly, it is worthwhile having a stab at the entities contained in it. Student, Course and Module seem definite candidates. The rest of the data items seem to be attributes of Student or Module or both.

The data model

An initial attempt at the data model might well be as shown in Figure 7.6.

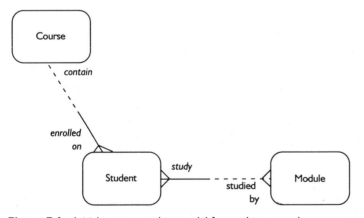

Figure 7.6 Initial attempt at data model for student records system

As we learned in the last chapter, however, we have to resolve the many-to-many relationship and modify the model as in Figure 7.7.

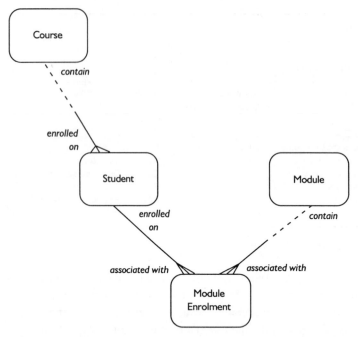

Figure 7.7   Data model for student records system, with many-to-many resolved

But is this correct? We have used common sense and, possibly, intuition to arrive at this. Let us go about this more systematically and *normalize* the data. We will go through this one step at a time.

Un-normalized Form (UNF)

The first step in normalization is to *write the data in Un-normalized Form* (UNF) as shown in Figure 7.8. For the moment, do not worry about the 1NF, 2NF and 3NF columns. The purpose of these will become clear as we go along.

You will notice that the UNF column contains the data item names for all the data items in the document. The first one, Student Number, is underlined because this has been chosen as the *key attribute* for this document. The key uniquely identifies the data and as each document is produced for *one and only one* student, the Student Number is a good choice of key.

The first four attributes start in the same column position and are given a UNF level number of 1. After the fourth attribute, the rest are indented slightly and given a UNF level of 2. This is because the document contains a *repeating group* of data.

UNF	UNF LEVEL	INF	2NF	3NF
Student Number	1			
Student Name	1			
Course Code	1			
Course Title	1			
Module Code	2			
Module Title	2			
No. of Credits	2			
Grade Point	2			
Result Code	2			
Result	2			

Figure 7.8 Student transcript – un-normalized

For a given value of the Student Code, the module data repeats giving several lines, one for each module. Of course, the Student Name, Course Code and Course Title do not repeat for a given Student Number; they can only have one value for each student and so they have a UNF level number of 1.

After writing out the data in un-normalized form in this way, the next stage is to *remove the repeating groups*.

First Normal Form (1NF)

The repeating group of data is largely to do with modules. The first step is to pick a key for the repeating data (i.e. each line of the module data) which uniquely identifies each line *within* the document. The obvious choice is Module Code. First Normal Form is then derived by separating out the repeating data as shown in Figure 7.9.

UNF	UNF LEVEL	INF	2NF	3NF
Student Number	1	Student Number		
Student Name	1	Student Name		
Course Code	1	Course Code		
Course Title	1	Course Title		
Module Code	2			
Module Title	2	Student Number		
No. of Credits	2	Module Code		
Grade Point	2	Module Title		
Result Code	2	No. of Credits		
Result	2	Grade Point		
		Result Code		
		Result		

Figure 7.9 Student transcript – First Normal Form

What has happened here? We have ended up with two groups of data items, which you can see are the starting points for evolution into entities. All the UNF level 1 items are taken across to 1NF together and here you can see the beginnings of a Student entity. The repeating data is taken out separately and given the key of Module Code, but the *first key*, Student Number, *is taken down with it*. This is a *compound key* and is made up of two or more *simple* keys. Basically, if the Student Number were not part of the key of the second group of data items, we would have student data and module data and no link between the two. The Student Number in the compound key provides the link between the two groups of data items.

In First Normal Form, you remove repeating groups of data.

Second Normal Form (2NF)

In second normal form, we *look at groups of data items that have more than one element to the key*. In other words, we look at compound keys (there is another type of key called a composite or hierarchic key and we will deal with this later).

Basically, we look at each of the non-key attributes and see if they really depend upon both of the elements of the compound key or just one of them. The group of data items we are to examine is shown below:

Student Number
Module Code
Module Title
No. of Credits
Grade Point
Result Code
Result

Let us look at each of the non-key attributes in turn.

- Module Title is obviously an attribute of a Module entity and has really got nothing to do with the Student Number. Hence, we say that Module Title is *determined by* Module Code.
- No. of Credits refers to the size of the module and hence is also determined by Module Code.
- Grade Point is the grade a particular Student gets for a particular Module; hence we need both keys to determine Grade Point.
- Result Code is the code for the result a particular Student gets for a particular Module and again needs both keys.
- Result is similar to Result Code at this stage of the normalization process.

The normalization table up to 2NF is given in Figure 7.10. We now seem to have a Student entity, a Module entity and a link entity which is the one with the compound key. Another word for these groups of data items is a *relation* and we will define this term a little later.

In Second Normal Form, you remove data items which depend on only part of a key.

UNF	UNF LEVEL	INF	2NF	3NF
Student Number	1	Student Number	Student Number	
Student Name	1	Student Name	Student Name	
Course Code	1	Course Code	Course Code	
Course Title	1	Course Title	Course Title	
Module Code	2			
Module Title	2	Student Number	Student Number	
No. of Credits	2	Module Code	Module Code	
Grade Point	2	Module Title	Grade Point	
Result Code	2	No. of Credits	Result Code	
Result	2	Grade Point	Result	
		Result Code		
		Result	Module Code	
			Module Title	
			No. of Credits	

Figure 7.10   Student transcript – Second Normal Form

Third Normal Form (3NF)

In Third Normal Form, we *look at all the attributes and see if they are really dependent upon the key.* If not, we decide upon a more suitable choice of key for these attributes.

In our example, there are two such questionable attributes: Course Title obviously really depends upon Course Code and Result really depends upon Result Code. In other words a Course Code has only one Course Title and a Result Code has only one Result. We take these two groups of data items out in 3NF and end up with the table shown in Figure 7.11.

You will notice that the keys of the groups taken out are also left behind as foreign keys (marked with an asterisk) to maintain the link between the entities. We have ended up with five entities, which is one more than our first stab at the problem. The extra entity is the one with a key of Result Code; this is really a simple look-up table. We will give each of these entities the following names: Student, Course, Module Enrolment, Result Code and Module. The name of the entity with the compound key, Module Enrolment, reflects the fact that both Student and Module are involved

UNF	UNF LEVEL	INF	2NF	3NF
Student Number	1	Student Number	Student Number	Student Number
Student Name	1	Student Name	Student Name	Student Name
Course Code	1	Course Code	Course Code	*Course Code
Course Title	1	Course Title	Course Title	
Module Code	2			Course Code
Module Title	2	Student Number	Student Number	Course Title
No. of Credits	2	Module Code	Module Code	
Grade Point	2	Module Title	Grade Point	Student Number
Result Code	2	No. of Credits	Result Code	Module Code
Result	2	Grade Point	Result	Grade Point
		Result Code		*Result Code
		Result	Module Code	
			Module Title	Result Code
			No. of Credits	Result
				Module Code
				Module Title
				No. of Credits

Figure 7.11   Student transcript – Third Normal Form

in this entity. You often find that compound key entities are difficult to name as they contain data relating to more than one entity.

In Third Normal Form, you remove any attributes which are not directly dependent upon the key.

We have ended up with a set of entities or *tables* which are said to be well-normalized. This is normally as far as we need to go. There is a Fourth Normal Form and a Fifth Normal Form but these are rarely found, especially if the first three stages have been done properly.

Third Normal Form tests

There are a couple of tests which we can apply to check whether the relations really are in Third Normal Form:

Test 1.   For each of the non-key attributes, is there just one possible value for a given value of the key?

For the majority of the non-key attributes the answer is obviously *yes*. For example, one Course Code can only have one Course Title and one Student Number and

Module Code together can only have one Grade Point. However, the foreign key Course Code in the Student entity makes you stop and think. Is a student only allowed to be on one course? In this sort of situation, you have to go back to the system users and ask them! In this case the answer is *yes* and so everything is all right. If the answer were *no*, the data model would become a lot more complicated as Student to Course would be many-to-many and you would have to check that the Modules studied were for the correct Course and so on.

Test 2. Do all of the non-key attributes depend *directly* upon the key?

Again, in this case, the answer is *yes* for all the non-key attributes. However, because we only normalize a sub-set of the complete system data when we analyse a document, it is often the case that a non-key field *really* depends upon another key. For example, if we wished to record a student's tutor for a particular module in the above normalization, we may well have ended up including it in the compound key entity as follows:

Student Number

Module Code

Grade Point

*Result Code

Tutor Name

However, strictly speaking, the tutor is really determined by the Tutor Group of which the student is a part and so should be removed from this entity and placed in another one for Tutor Group. The Student will also be linked to this Tutor Group. This example will be developed fully in the section on composite keys later in the chapter. This is a case of *transitive dependence*, in which an attribute does have a unique value for a given key but is *really* dependent on another key which is itself dependent on the first key.

Construction of Third Normal Form (3NF) data structure

A data structure for these entities can now be constructed as in Figure 7.12. It is easy to see the pattern here. The individual elements of the compound key become the many end of a one-to-many relationship with the entities that have those elements as their simple keys. Entities with foreign keys become the many end of a one-to-many relationship with the entity which has this foreign key as its simple key. This is a bit complicated to put in writing and it is useful to think of this visually.

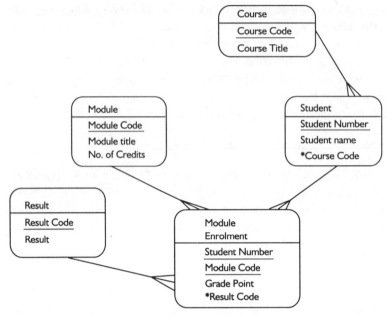

Figure 7.12 Student records system – data structure based upon student transcript Third Normal Form

The crow's foot can be thought of as a *grab* and the simple keys *grab* the asterisk of a foreign key and also *grab* any compound keys of which they are a part. Notice, that unlike the data models we built in the last chapter, we omit optionality and relationship names in the 3NF data structure. These will be added at a later time (see Section 7.6).

Summary of stages of normalization

- Write out data in Un-normalized Form (UNF).
- Convert to First Normal Form (1NF) by separating repeating groups.
- Convert to Second Normal Form (2NF) by separating data items which depend on only part of a key.
- Convert to Third Normal Form (3NF) by separating any attributes not directly dependent upon the key, i.e. those which depend upon other non-key attributes instead.
- Apply the Third Normal Form tests.
- Construct the Third Normal Form data structure.

You may find it useful to remember the following memory jogger when creating First, Second and Third Normal Forms:

- repeating groups;
- part-key dependencies;
- non-key dependencies.

7.2.3 The module class list

It is possible, in fact very likely, that the same data used in the student transcript example would be used to produce other documents for other users of the system. The previous example contained data presented for the benefit of the student. The module leader might well want the same data but presented in a different way; for example a module class list as in Figure 7.13.

You can see that the module class list in Figure 7.13 contains most of the data in the previous example, but some extra data has been added and a little has been missed out. For example, the code and name of the module leader is included. The module leader is a lecturer and a lecturer can take on several roles, e.g. module leader, personal tutor, course leader or simply a tutor who supports the module leader. However, in the system, a lecturer is stored under Lecturer Code and the exact roles of the lecturer need to be shown. You will also notice that the document only contains the Result Code and not the Result description. This is because the

---

Module Code: COM120
Module Title: Systems Analysis
Number of Credits: 20
Lecturer Code of Module Leader: MLEJ
Lecturer Name of Module Leader: Mark Lejk

Student Number	Student Name	Course Code	Course Title	Grade Point	Resullt Code
0156786	Simon Adams	G105	BA Business Computing	9	P
9876455	Jennifer Barker	G105	BA Business Computing	3	RE
2341235	James Bull	G106	BSc Computing	2	RCE
3493426	Deborah Cameron	G105	BA Business Computing	15	P
.	.	.	.	.	.
.	.	.	.	.	.
4561239	Susan Williams	G108	BSc Information Technology	3	DC

Total number of students: 76

Figure 7.13 The module class list

module leaders deal with Result Codes frequently and know what each one means. Finally, this document includes a total for the number of students on the module. Normalization of this document produces the result shown in Figure 7.14: ML stands for Module Leader.

If you compare this normalization to the previous one, you can see that the final 3NF entities are virtually the same and any differences are owing to those we have introduced to the data in the first place. So, the Course and Student entities are identical to the first normalization. In the Module Enrolment entity, the compound keys have the elements Student Number and Module Code in a different sequence but they are still the same. Also, Result Code is not marked as a foreign key in the second normalization as the Result Description is not present in the document. A new entity, Lecturer has been introduced together with a foreign key in Module which links to it.

The other new thing to come out of this is that the No. of Students disappears in Third Normal Form. This is because the attribute can be *calculated* by adding up the number of students on a module and, therefore, need not be stored.

As we go through a system, normalizing inputs and outputs, it is always the case that not all the data items for each entity will appear on each input or output. We have to rationalize the entities as new data items determined by the same key crop up, and we gradually collect together the complete set of data items for each key.

UNF	UNF LEVEL	1NF	2NF	3NF
Module Code	1	Module Code	Module Code	Module Code
Module Title	1	Module Title	Module Title	Module Title
No. of Credits	1	No. of Credits	No. of Credits	No. of Credits
Lec Code of ML	1	Lec Code of ML	Lec Code of ML	*Lec Code of ML
Name of ML	1	Name of ML	Name of ML	
No. of students	1	No. of students	No. of students	Lecturer Code
Student Number	2			Lecturer Name
Student Name	2	Module Code	Module Code	
Course Code	2	Student Number	Student Number	Module Code
Course Title	2	Student Name	Grade Point	Student Number
Grade Point	2	Course Code	Result Code	Grade Point
Result Code	2	Course Title		Result Code
		Grade Point	Student Number	
		Result Code	Student Name	Student Number
			Course Code	Student Name
			Course Title	*Course Code
				Course Code
				Course Title

Figure 7.14   The normalized class list

However, the main point to come out of this is that, from whichever point we start the normalization, the final Third Normal Form entities should be the same. This is why the technique is so powerful and so frequently used.

If we combine the results of the two normalizations we have done so far, we end up with the 3NF data structure in Figure 7.15. You can see that this structure will get more and more detailed with new entities appearing and new data attributes added as further inputs and outputs are normalized. Hence, normalization is known as a *bottom-up* and rigorous technique compared to logical data modelling which is very much a *top-down*, intuitive and subjective technique.

7.2.4 Normalization and relational data analysis

Normalization is the only part of the larger subject of relational data analysis (RDA) which we cover in this book. Relational data analysis has its origins in set theory and is based on the work of Codd in the early 1970s. We do not intend to go into the theory of RDA, but there are several good books which deal with the subject in some depth.

A relation is a term which describes a table of data items and, for our purposes, is the same as an entity. You will hear the words relation, table and entity used

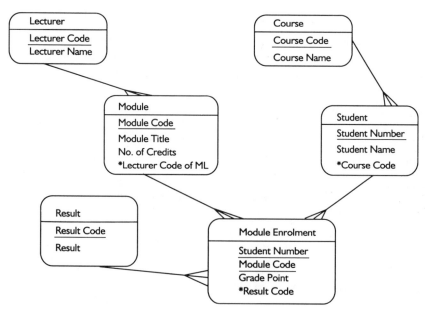

Figure 7.15 Student records system – 3NF data structure based upon student transcript and module class list

Student Number	Student Name	Course Code
0156786	Simon Adams	G105
9876455	Jennifer Barker	G105
2341235	James Bull	G106
3493426	Deborah Cameron	G105
.	.	.
.	.	.
4561239	Susan Williams	G106

Figure 7.16 The student relation

interchangeably in systems analysis. An example of a relation taken from our second example is the Student relation as shown in Figure 7.16.

There are several rules which apply to relations, but the main ones are as follows:

1. The order of the rows must not be significant.
2. The order of the columns must not be significant.
3. Each row must be unique.
4. Each column must have only one value per row.

By applying normalization, we end up with a set of relations. The advantage of organizing our data in this way is that we remove data duplication. A Student Name is only stored *once* in the Student relation and is stored alongside the *key attribute* of that student which is the Student Number. The only times a data item appears more than once is when they act as *links*, either as a foreign key or part of a compound key.

By storing a data item once only, we also ensure data integrity. If the Student Name were to appear in more than one place, it would be possible for the same Student to have two different names (possibly due to spelling mistakes). This may sound far-fetched, but as far as a computer system is concerned the difference between Williams and Wiliams is the same as between Adam and Kublai Khan!

Basically, we end up with a *tidy* data set consisting of relations each with its own key and containing attributes which are determined by only that key. The relations are linked via foreign keys and compound keys.

7.3 Normalization of tables of data

So far, we have normalized individual documents, in which each document has a unique key. Documents such as these frequently act as inputs and outputs to computer systems. However, reports in the form of tables of data are also frequently produced by computer systems, and these reports may actually summarize several of the documents which we have just mentioned. We will now have a look at how you normalize such a table of data. The table in Figure 7.17 is required as output from our computer system.

Course Code	Course Title	Module Code	Module Title	Lec Code of ML	Lec Name of ML	Mod. Type Code	Module Type Description
G105	BA Business Computing	COM220	Database Systems	SSTI	Sue Stirk	C	Core
		COM221	Systems Analysis	MLEJ	Mark Lejk	C	Core
		COM228	Desk Top Publishing	MMCA	Moira McAllister	O	Option
		COM245	Organizational Study	MLEJ	Mark Lejk	O	Option
G104	HND Computer Studies	COM220	Database Systems	SSTI	Sue Stirk	C	Core
		COM221	Systems Analysis	MLEJ	Mark Lejk	C	Core
		COM228	Desk Top Publishing	MMCA	Moira McAllister	O	Option
		COM245	Organizational Study	MLEJ	Mark Lejk	O	Option
G106	B.Sc. Computing	COM220	Database Systems	SSTI	Sue Stirk	C	Core
		COM221	Systems Analysis	MLEJ	Mark Lejk	O	Option
		COM228	Desk Top Publishing	MMCA	Moira McAllister	E	Elective
		COM245	Organizational Study	MLEJ	Mark Lejk	E	Elective

Figure 7.17   Output required from system

The table shows each course, the modules in each course, whether these modules are core, optional or elective for each course, and details of the module leader for each module. The only real difference between this table and the sorts of documents we have met so far is that the table itself does not have a unique key, but is a collection of sets of data which do have a unique key. It is as if several individual documents, one for each course, were combined together. Therefore, we treat the set of course data as our starting point for normalization and give the un-normalized data a key of Course Code as in the normalization table shown in Figure 7.18.

UNF	UNF LEVEL	1NF	2NF	3NF
Course Code	1	Course Code	Course Code	Course Code
Course Title	1	Course Title	Course Title	Course Title
Module Code	2			
Module Title	2	Course Code	Course Code	Course Code
Lec Code of ML	2	Module Code	Module Code	Module Code
Name of ML	2	Module Title	Mod Type Code	*Mod Type Code
Mod Type Code	2	Lec Code of ML	Mod Type Desc	
Mod Type Desc	2	Name of ML		Mod Type Code
		Mod Type Code	Module Code	Mod Type Desc
		Mod Type Desc	Module Title	
			Lec Code of ML	Module Code
			Name of ML	Module Title
				*Lec Code of ML
				Lecturer Code
				Lecturer Name

Figure 7.18   The normalized table

Apart from the starting point, this is exactly the same as when we normalized the previous documents. As can be seen in Figure 7.19, however, we now have two more entities to add to our 3NF data structure, i.e. Module Type and Course/Module Link. You can see our data structure getting bigger and bigger as we normalize more and more data.

7.4 Composite keys

7.4.1 Like a compound key, but not quite

So far, we have met three types of key. A *simple* key is a single data item which by itself determines the non-key attributes in an entity. Examples of these are Student Number in the Student entity, Course Code in the Course entity and Module Code in the Module entity.

A *compound* key contains two or more other keys all of which are needed together to determine the non-key attributes in an entity. Most often these other keys are themselves simple keys. Examples of compound keys are Course Code with Module Code in the Course/Module Link entity and Student Number with Module Code in the Module Enrolment entity.

A *foreign* key is not really a key as such. It is a non-key attribute in one entity which is a key attribute in another. Examples of foreign keys are Module Type Code in the Course/Module entity and Lecturer Code (Module Leader) in the Module Entity.

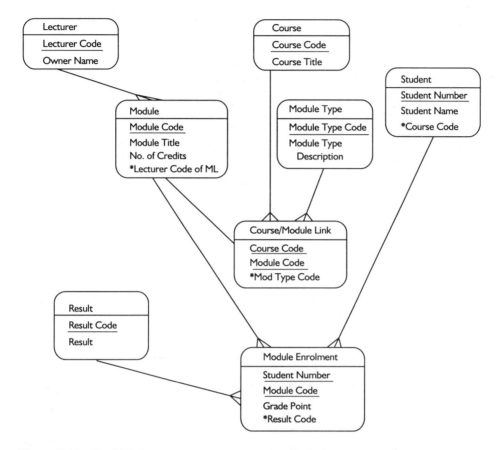

Figure 7.19 The 3NF data structure with entities Module Type and Course/Module Link

There is another type of key which occurs quite frequently and is often confused with a compound key. This type of key is called a *composite* or *hierarchic* key and is subtly different to a compound key. We will introduce this type of key through an example.

7.4.2 The tutor group class list

We have already met Modules and module leaders. When a module is actually taught, students are split into tutorial groups, each group having a tutor. The module leader will normally act as tutor for some of these groups but other tutors will take some groups so that the module is taught by a team of tutors led by the module leader. Tutorial groups are timetabled at different times in different rooms and our computer system is required to produce a class list of students in each tutorial group. The tutor group class list looks like the document in Figure 7.20.

Module Code: COM120	Tutor Group Number: 3
Module Title: Systems Analysis	Day: Wednesday
Lecturer Code (Module Leader): MLEJ	Time: 10.00 –11.30
Lecturer Name (Module Leader): Mark Lejk	Room: SP304
	Lecturer Code (Tutor): DDEE
	Lecturer Name (Tutor): Dave Deeks

Student Number	Student Name
0156786	Simon Adams
9876455	Jennifer Barker
2341235	James Bull
3493426	Deborah Cameron
.	.
.	.
4561239	Susan Williams

Figure 7.20   The tutor group class list

First of all, a word of caution! Documents such as this can be deceptive. One of the problems with normalization is that it can be too easy to simply follow the rules and not really understand what it is you are doing. Although this document covers only one tutorial group, it is obvious that a module will have more than one tutorial group. In other words, we have a *repeating group* of tutorial groups within a module. On top of that we have a *repeating group* of students within a tutorial group! Hence we have a *nested repeating group* – a repeating group within a repeating group.

That is not all. We are obviously going to have an entity called Tutor Group sometime soon. What is the key of this entity? Tutor Group Number? No, each module is going to have its own Tutor Groups and a Tutor Group Number of 3 is not enough to identify a particular Tutor Group as it may be the third Tutor Group in the systems analysis module or the software engineering module or any other module. In other words, Tutor Group Number is not unique and needs to be qualified by the Module Code to make it unique. The key of Tutor Group is written as follows:

(Module Code)

(Tutor Group Number)

The brackets mean that the lower level non-unique attribute Tutor Group Number must be qualified by the higher level unique attribute Module Code to make the whole key unique. It looks like a compound key, doesn't it? But it is different.

7.4.3 The special nature of the composite key

Consider a compound key we have met already:

Student Number

Module Code

These two keys are put together to determine data associated with both a Student and a Module i.e. the student's grade and result in a module. Both Student Number and Module Code are unique keys in their own right – one Student Number is the key for one and only one Student and one Module Code is the key for one and only one Module. But as already mentioned, in the example we are considering now one Tutor Group Number is not the key for one and only one Tutor Group but for a range of Tutor Groups in different modules, and this is what makes the key a composite rather than a compound. Many students of data analysis find this concept difficult and it is worth taking your time reading this until you understand it.

7.4.4 Normalizing the tutor group class list

All of this may well seem complicated. To an extent it is, but to help you get the idea we will show you the fully normalized version of the class list (Figure 7.21) and then demonstrate how we arrived at it. We hope that it will all become clear.

UNF	UNF LEVEL	1NF	2NF	3NF
Module Code	1	Module Code	Module Code	Module Code
Module Title	1	Module Title	Module Title	Module Title
Lec Code of ML	1	Lec Code of ML	Lec Code of ML	*Lec Code of ML
Lec Name of ML	1	Lec Name of ML	Lec Name of ML	
Tutor Group No.	2			Lecturer Code
Day	2	(Module Code)	(Module Code)	Lecturer Name
Time	2	(Tutor Group No.)	(Tutor Group No.)	
Room	2	Day	Day	(Module Code)
Lec Code of Tutor	2	Time	Time	(Tutor Group No.)
Name of Tutor	2	Room	Room	Day
Student Number	3	Lec Code of Tutor	Lec Code of Tutor	Time
Student Name	3	Name of Tutor	Name of Tutor	Room
				*Lec Code of Tutor
		(Module Code)	(Module Code)	
		(Tutor Group No.)	(Tutor Group No.)	(Module Code)
		Student Number	Student Number	(Tutor Group No.)
		Student Name		Student Number
			Student Number	
			Student Name	(Module Code)
				(Tutor Group No.)
				Student Number
				Student Number
				Student Name

Figure 7.21   The normalized class list

There is so much of interest here that it is difficult to know where to start – so we will start at the beginning. We have already mentioned the nested repeating groups and you can see how these are written in the UNF column with the different tiers being given increasing UNF level numbers of 1, 2 and 3.

When we go to 1NF, we have to remove repeating groups *twice* because they are nested. The first time we end up with details about the Tutor Group with a composite key of

(Module Code)

(Tutor Group No.)

and the second time we get details of allocation of students to the tutorial groups with the following key:

(Module Code)

(Tutor Group No.)

Student Number

This is starting to look quite complex, but it is really a compound key made up from the composite key and a simple key (Student Number).

In 2NF we examine this last compound key and remove the Student details into another relation. We are left behind with this three-part key on its own with no non-key attributes to determine. However, we cannot and should not get rid of this as it acts as the only link between Student and Tutor Group. It is called a *key-only relation*.

In 3NF, we take out the Lecturer details, but we do it twice, once for the Module Leader and once for the Tutor. We will end up here with *two* links from Lecturer, one to the Module and one to the Tutor Group, to represent the two different roles of the lecturer as module leader and as tutor. If we join these relations together, we get the structure in Figure 7.22.

The composite keys need a mention here. When linking a composite key to other relations, you mark the top-level unique key (in this case Module Code) as a foreign key and then link it like any other foreign key. You will notice the asterisk to the left of Module Code in the Tutor Group relation marking it as a foreign key. The key of Tutor Group Allocation is really a compound key made up of the composite key and the simple key (Student Number). It is, hence, linked to the entities which have these two elements as their total key, i.e. Tutor Group and Student.

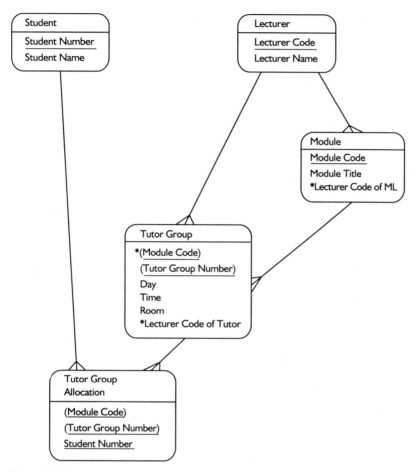

Figure 7.22   Third Normal Form data structure for class list

7.5 Combining the 3NF data structures

If we now combine this last data structure with the one we produced at the end of Section 7.3, we arrive at the structure shown in Figure 7.23. The data structure just contains the names of the relations so as not confuse the overall picture with unnecessary detail.

By normalizing only four different sets of data it has been possible to produce quite a complicated data structure.

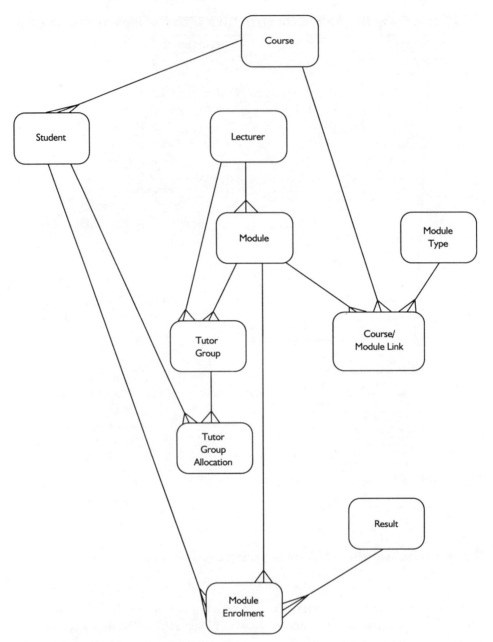

Figure 7.23   Combined 3NF data structure

7.6 Comparing the 3NF data structure with the logical data model

7.6.1 Aiming for the definitive data model

You can see how normalization takes you into the heart of the system. It forces you to take a detailed analytical approach and is invaluable in arriving at a *correct* data model. However, the data structure produced does not show optionality or show what the relationships actually mean. This sort of angle was taken in producing the logical data model. We need to combine the two to get the *best* data model for the system. You can be pretty sure that normalization has thrown up some entities that did not appear in the logical data model.

7.6.2 The logical data model

Imagine that at the end of the logical data modelling described in the last chapter, a systems analyst had come up with the data model in Figure 7.24. You can see that this is a lot simpler than the 3NF data structure produced at the end of the last section – the analyst has made a number of omissions and mistakes which we can

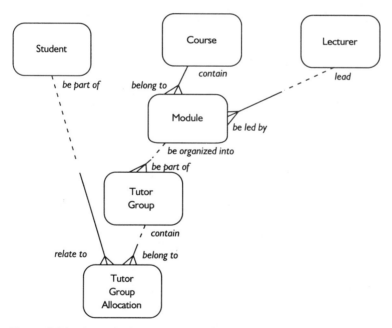

Figure 7.24 An analyst's attempt at a data model

now see that normalization has brought to light. For example, the analyst has assumed that a Module can only belong to one Course, whereas we now know it can belong to more than one. The analyst has not realized that the system needs to store the Lecturer Code of the Tutor for a Tutor Group. The entities Module Type and Result do not appear in the data model simply because the analyst has not thought of them as entities, even though, strictly speaking, they are.

Finally, the analyst has not linked Student to Module, but has tried to be clever and linked them via Tutor Group Allocation. Although this may seem reasonable, the module leader needs to know which Students have been enrolled on the Module *before* Students are allocated to Tutor Groups. So the link must be there because of the time delay. Also, if the number of Students enrolled is not great, they may be only one Tutor Group, in which case the module leader will act as tutor and the Tutor Group and Tutor Group Allocation entities are not really needed.

Normalization provides the mechanistic framework to sort out the data properly, but the analyst still needs to understand the system in the ways illustrated in the previous paragraph to make the final data model realistic.

7.6.3 Combining the two views

Combining the two views may well produce the final data model in Figure 7.25.

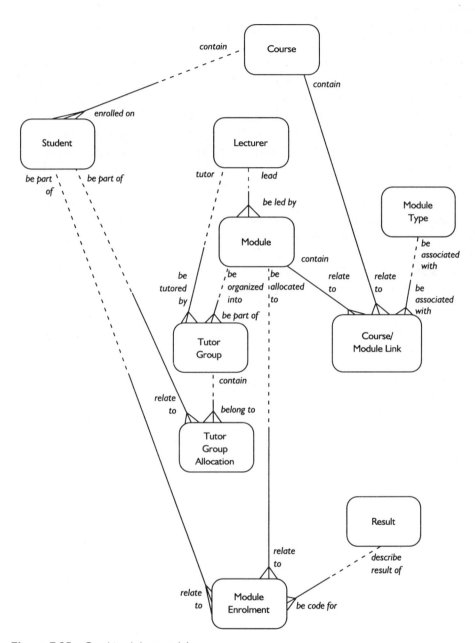

Figure 7.25 Combined data model

Summary

This chapter began by examining the meaning of a relationship in data analysis. It then introduced the concept of normalization by slowly introducing you to the three stages: First, Second and Third Normal Forms. We then looked at the Third Normal Form tests and how you construct a data structure from Third Normal Form relations. You then saw how composite or hierarchical keys differ from compound keys and how a Third Normal Form data structure is reconciled with a logical data model.

You may have realized by now that normalization and data modelling are huge subjects and the models can get very complicated. However, computer systems nowadays *are* complicated and you can only expect them to become more so. Modern databases can be absolutely enormous and it is not unusual to find systems with more than a hundred entities. In order to tackle these systems, you need a methodical proven technique which is based on sound theoretical principles. Normalization is such a technique. Use it correctly and you will not regret it.

Further reading

C. J. Date, *An Introduction to Database Systems*, 6th edn, Addison-Wesley, Reading, MA, 1995.

Logicalization of DFDs

8.1 Introduction

8.1.1 Reminders about DFDs

Data Flow Diagrams (DFDs) have been found to be an extremely useful systems analysis tool. Not only do they allow the analyst to get a structured view of a system, but they are also an excellent communication vehicle between the analyst and the user. Because they are pictures, and a 'picture is worth a thousand words', users pretty soon get the hang of them and quite often go away and draw their own versions.

We first met DFDs in Chapter 2 and continued through to Chapter 5, by which time we had expanded to the lowest level the processes which they contain. All of the DFDs we had seen up to that stage modelled an existing physical system. These were called *current physical DFDs*. We saw that they were extremely useful diagrams as they describe the system as it is and make no attempt to make any improvements or changes to it.

In practice, however, systems evolve over time. It is often the case that the people who first started running a system move on and are replaced by new people with different ideas who make changes to the system. Several such changes take place over time, and a system may be quite different from its original version. If these changes are not co-ordinated, we can end up with a piecemeal set of procedures whose intentions are not particularly clear. Often, when investigating why a particular procedure is undertaken, the answer is 'because it's been done like this since I started working here and I've just carried on in the same way'.

8.1.2 Why logicalize?

So, a system which does not fully reflect what the system was originally intended to do may be in operation. As a result, by examining a system and documenting it physically, the *policy* behind the system may not be obvious. You often hear the expression 'I can't see the wood for the trees'. This is particularly pertinent in systems analysis. The analyst is confronted with a lot of sometimes detailed procedures many of which are inter-linked, and it is difficult to see the overall picture – what is the system *really* trying to do. The *physical* circumstances are masking what is *logically* going on.

Early in Chapter 2 we introduced the idea of being able to take either a physical or a logical view of a situation: it is now time to introduce how DFDs can assist in this. Logicalization is a very powerful and sophisticated technique for unravelling a physical system and expressing it logically. At the end of the technique, we end up with a *logical DFD* of the *current* system which tells us what the system is doing and reflects the *policy* behind the current system. The *current physical DFD* tells us how that policy is implemented.

Logicalization is often regarded as difficult by practising systems analysts and some actually avoid doing it. This is a mistake as it often throws light on to a system which would have been missed otherwise. It is not a rigid technique, like normalization for example. It is more a set of guidelines which can be applied with a reasonable amount of flexibility. Not only does it supply a picture of the policy behind the existing system, it also highlights problem areas, establishes boundaries for future system development, and forms the basis or platform for the specification of the required system. In addition, it forces the analyst to start thinking logically and abstractly and to move away from the constraints imposed by the existing system. It is, hence, an empowering technique and very, very important.

8.1.3 Business Process Re-engineering (BPR)

Before we get on with the subject of logicalization, we want to pause for a moment and mention a concept that is becoming increasingly widely publicized and which we feel is appropriate at this point. The term business process re-engineering in fact covers three distinctly different management approaches, i.e. process improvement, process re-design and process re-engineering. *Improvement* is the least radical, with improvements tending to be small but on-going, confined within existing boundaries and focussing on improvements to the existing system. *Re-design* is more fundamental and in reality represents the majority use of the term BPR. It goes beyond improving existing processes, and asks the question 'should we be doing this at all?' *Re-engineering* describes the most radical re-think. It sets targets, aiming for extremely dramatic improvements such as cutting order to delivery times from one month to one day and reducing costs by 70% whilst at the same time improving service levels by specified amounts. The common thread to all BPR however is the attempt to improve, rationalize, replace or simply do away with, processes.

You may notice that we introduced BPR by referring to it as a concept. It is *not* a technique. It is simply an idea, an approach, a statement of intent. We are mentioning it here because the analyst who understands processes, who is used to identifying them and describing them, diagramming them, is in a very strong position when it comes to unravelling them, re-organizing them and *re-engineering* them.

Processes are, of course, the fundamental part of the data flow diagram, and the ability to logicalize such a diagram can prove to be extremely valuable to analysts who find themselves in a BPR environment. The likelihood of this happening is increasing steadily and, thus, so is the possibility of the systems analyst taking a key role in turning management objectives into tangible designs for discussion.

8.2 Steps in logicalization

8.2.1 The example – a return to the student assessment system

As usual, we will explain this technique by going through an example. We will return to the student assessment system which was introduced in Chapter 4 (*Creating DFDs*). At the end of that chapter, we concluded with a complete set of DFDs for the current physical system, which incorporated a level 1 DFD and level 2 DFDs for processes 1, 2 and 4. These are reproduced for reference in Figures 8.1–8.4. Process 3 in the level 1 DFD was considered unsuitable for expansion into level 2 and so was described using structured English and you will find this description in Figure 5.12. You will find an entity model for the current system in Figure 8.5. These diagrams together provide a description of the existing system expressed physically.

8.2.2 Step 1 – rationalization of data flows

This step is easy. Often, in physical systems, data floats around on pieces of paper with names like *pink top copy* or *yellow form*. Data is also often transmitted over the telephone by word of mouth. It is common to see data flows on physical DFDs with these names.

Rationalization of data flows involves replacing the physical data flow name with the data actually flowing. So, for example, the *pink top copy* may well contain order details and the name should hence be replaced by *order details*. In the student assessment system, most of the names of data flows are already rational or logical. Student marks are student marks whichever way you look at them. However, a candidate for change is the *stamped addressed envelope* provided by the student in order that the results can be sent out. When you really think about it, this is a request by the student for results. The stamped addressed envelope is the way this request is physically implemented. Hence, the data flow *stamped addressed envelope* should be replaced in the logical system by the data flow *request for results*.

8.2.3 Step 2 – rationalization of data stores

If you look again at Figures 8.1–8.4, you can see a number of data stores. All of these contain some of the data which is described in the entity model. For example the data store M1 is the Course document and contains the entities Course and Subject. Data store M1/1 (Subject results file) will contain parts of the entities Subject, Student and Module Enrolment.

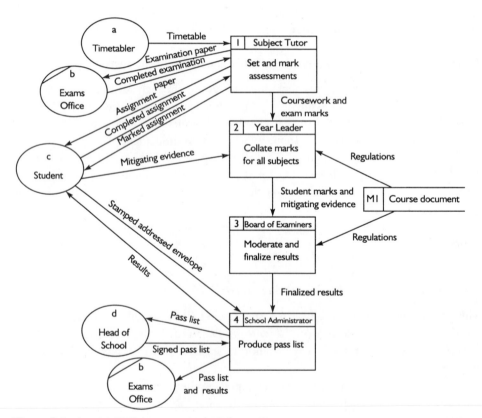

Figure 8.1   Level I DFD (current physical) for student assessment system

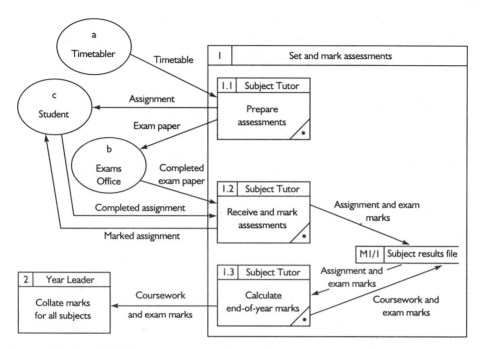

Figure 8.2 Level 2 DFD (current physical) for student assessment system process 1: Set and mark assessments

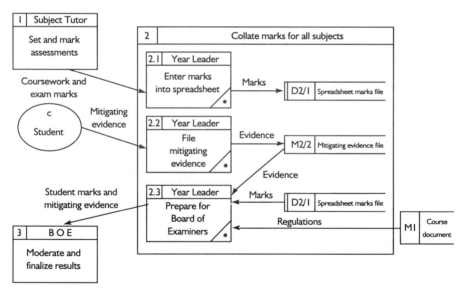

Figure 8.3 Level 2 DFD (current physical) for student assessment system process 2: Collate marks for all subjects

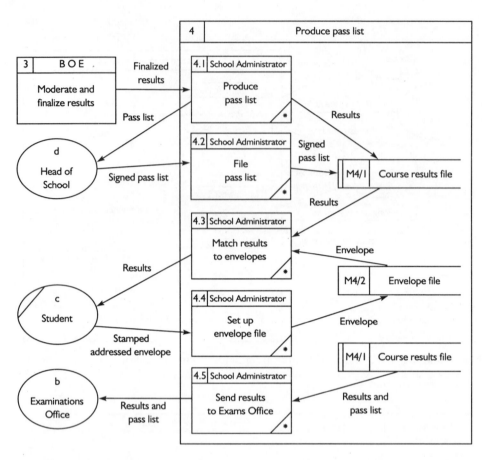

Figure 8.4   Level 2 DFD (current physical) for student assessment system process 4: Produce pass list

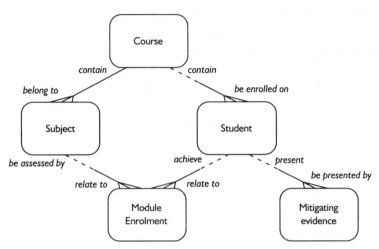

Figure 8.5   Entity model for current student assessment system

When we say *parts* of the entities, we mean that the data store may not contain all of the data items for each entity. So, for example, it is unlikely that the Subject Results File will contain details of students' addresses as it is really a record of marks gained by students in the different subjects. By looking at the data stores and entities in this way, we can construct a data store/entity cross-reference and this is shown in Figure 8.6 for the current physical system.

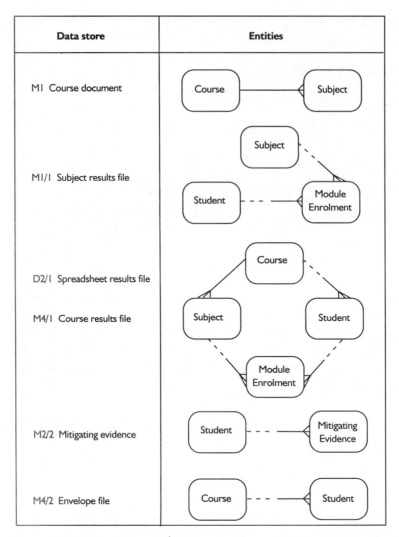

Data store	Entities
M1 Course document	
M1/1 Subject results file	
D2/1 Spreadsheet results file	
M4/1 Course results file	
M2/2 Mitigating evidence	
M4/2 Envelope file	

Figure 8.6 Physical data store/entity cross-reference for current physical system

You will see that the various entities are often stored in more than one file. Student, for example, appears in data stores M1/1, D2/1, M4/1, M2/2, M4/2. As already mentioned, each of these data stores will store *some* of the Student details but it may well be that the same data items are stored in more than one data store. In fact, M4/1 (Course results file) is really the same as D2/1 (Spreadsheet marks file). This happens frequently in physical systems. Data is often spread over several files because different people want access to different information. Data is frequently duplicated simply because people find it is easier to have a copy of a file in their office rather than having to go to a central location to look up information.

However these are *physical* reasons. From a logical point of view, the various parties involved simply need to access data. When we rationalize data stores, we remove this duplication so that an entity resides in *one and only one* data store. We are really preparing the way for a computerized system here by grouping data into logical groups, storing each logical group once only (a logical database) and giving anyone who wishes to access this data the ability to do so. In a computer system, this would be achieved by users having access to a central database through terminals. In a logical system, however, we simply say that the users have access to the data. How this is achieved is irrelevant.

It is usual to group the entities in the entity model into logical data stores. This is often quite difficult and, to be quite honest, different analysts do this in different ways. As a result, there is no *correct* way of doing it and students often find this situation unsatisfactory. As a rule of thumb, entities should be grouped together if they are functionally related – entities which are linked, operated on together, created together or part of the same major inputs or outputs to the system. It is often useful to group them together if they can be described by a single term, e.g. *sales ledger*.

Figure 8.7 shows our attempt at grouping the entities. We have decided to have *two* logical data stores. D1 is called Courses and contains details of Courses and the Subjects which make them up. D2 is called Students and contains details of Students, any Mitigating Evidence and Module Enrolments. It would have been equally

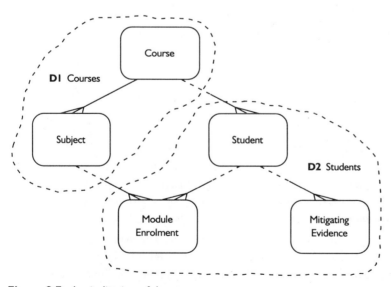

Figure 8.7 Logicalization of data stores

feasible to include the Module Enrolment entity in the Courses file, but we feel it belongs more to the Student than to the Course.

These two logical data stores replace all of the data stores on the physical DFD. We have replaced six data stores with two, which is a considerable achievement. It basically simplifies our view of the system and makes it more accessible and easy to understand. We are saying: 'This system and all of its files is really about Students enrolled on Courses'. It gives us a healthy perspective as to what the policy of the system is.

Before we finish this section, just a word about *transient data stores*. These are data stores that store data temporarily. Examples are in-trays or temporary files which are there simply because data is to be collected and then transferred in a batch at the end of a day for example. It is usual to remove these data stores in logicalization because they serve no logical purpose. They exist for a physical reason. However, sometimes they should be kept. This occurs when a subsequent process needs a whole batch of information before it can work effectively. An example would be a set of orders which are to be loaded on to vans for despatch. The mechanics of loading orders on to vans, which may well go to different destinations, can only be effectively done when details of all the orders are available. Hence, the transient data store which holds these order details should be carried across to the logical system as it is logically needed.

8.2.4 Step 3 – rationalization of bottom level processes

This is the most important step in logicalization and can often totally transform a system. There are several aspects to this step and we will go through them one at a time with reference to our student assessment system.

1. As the processes in the logical DFD are meant to be logical rather than physical, all reference to the location of the process or the responsibility for that process should be removed. Hence, the location/responsibility box will be blank.

2. A logical process should transform or use data simply because the system requires it to do so. How it is implemented is irrelevant. This applies to processes 4.3 and 4.4 in Figure 8.4 for example which deal with the setting up of an envelope file and subsequent matching of results to the names on the envelope. Process 4.4 *Set up envelope file* should become *Register request for results* and process 4.3 *Match results to envelope* should become *Output results to students*.

3. If a process is simply re-organizing data by sorting or collating then it should be removed. There are several examples of this in our system. Production and signing of a pass list is really presenting already existing data in a different form. So, processes 4.1 and 4.2 are no longer needed. Also, the job of a Year Leader is

largely one of collation. The Year Leader collects the marks from Subject Tutors and re-organizes these marks into a form suitable for the Board of Examiners. Hence, processes 2.1 and 2.3 are no longer needed.

4. Any processes which must remain clerical should be excluded from the DFD and replaced by an external entity. This does apply in our system. The preparation and marking of assignments by the Module Leader is not going to be considered for computerization. The Subject Tutor should become an external entity because it is not intended for the computer system to do this part of their job. It would be just about feasible for the Subject Tutor to set assessments on the computer and for the computer to mark these assessments and store the grades. However, this would be an ambitious and expensive project, and it is certainly not intended for this system. The Subject Tutor sets and marks assessments outside of the logical system and the system then stores the marks.

5. Where a process involves some subjective decision making, or involves an activity which is legally required to be done by a person, then the process, should be split. An external entity should be introduced to replace the relevant parts of the process and data flows introduced between the process and the external entity. This applies to process 3, where the Board of Examiners decides on the final results for students. Automating this process is equivalent to allowing a computer system to issue dismissal notices in a personnel system simply by looking at an employee's details and history. It is, in our opinion, one of the most over-looked aspects of computer systems and can lead to accusations of inhumanity and *the computer taking over*. In process 3, the Board of Examiners looks at student results, takes into account any mitigating evidence and arrives at a consensus decision. Automating this process is extremely dangerous and, some would argue, immoral.

6. Where a process is retrieving data only to display or print it, then it should be considered for removal. However, if it is considered to be a major part of the system's functionality, it should be retained. This applies to the sending of results to students and the Exams Office. We have decided to keep this as it is an important part of the system.

The following aspects should also be considered when rationalizing processes, but there are no relevant examples in our system:

7. If a process is simply passing data to another process without transforming it, then it should be removed and replaced by a data flow.

8. Where two or more processes are always performed together they should be combined.

9. Where two or more processes are performing exactly the same function, they should be combined.

8.2.5 Step 4 – reconstruction of the DFD

This is where it gets interesting. Several of our lower level processes have been removed. A number of external entities have been introduced to replace part or all of some processes and we have drastically changed our data stores. We now need to re-group our lower level processes into new level 1 processes. This is not easy, and requires a combination of applying an overall view with a detailed look at what the lower level processes are actually doing. A level 1 logical DFD of the current system can be found in Figure 8.8.

The first thing to notice is that the logical DFD is a lot simpler than the physical one. This is as it should be. If the logical DFD is more complicated than the physical, it is likely that you have made a mistake. Basically, the logical DFD is telling us that the system stores student marks and mitigating evidence (process 1), supplies this information to the Board of Examiners and records the Board's decisions (process 3), and then outputs this information to interested parties (process 2). To assist in this processing two logical data stores are used, one of which stores student details and the other course details.

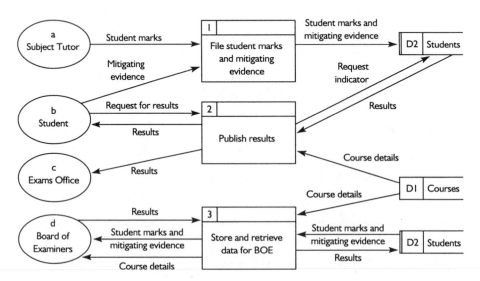

Figure 8.8   Level 1 logical DFD of current student assessment system

8.3 A further example

To help you get the idea of logicalization we are now going to look at the other example from Chapter 4: the company called Marine Construction. We will begin by reproducing again in Figures 8.9–8.12 the complete set of DFDs for the current physical system.

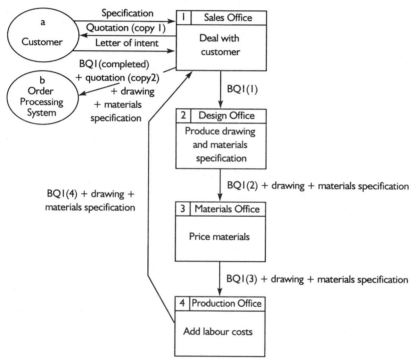

Figure 8.9   Level 1 physical DFD for Marine Construction

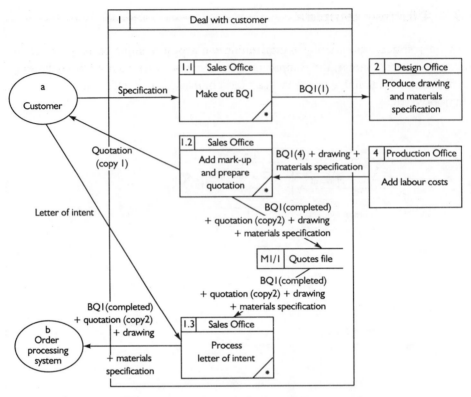

Figure 8.10   Level 2 DFD for Marine Construction Sales Office

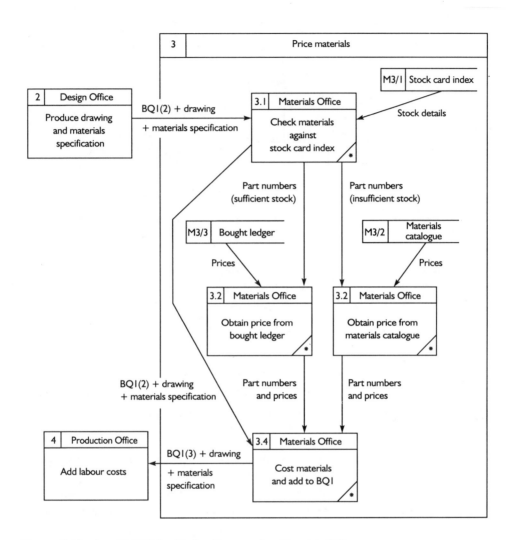

Figure 8.11 Level 2 DFD for Marine Construction Materials Office

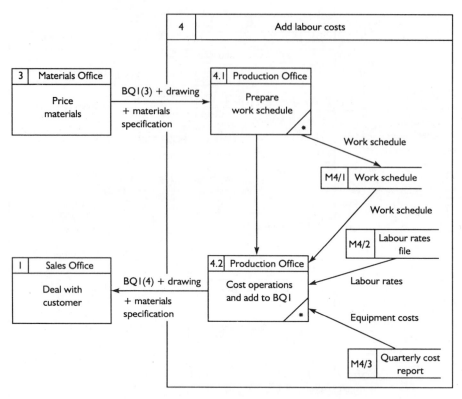

Figure 8.12   Level 2 DFD for Marine Construction Production Office

The level 1 logical DFD for the same system is shown in Figure 8.13. As the original system description is rather sparse, certain assumptions have been made and it is the main thrust of the logicalization process which we wish to get across. Look at the DFD carefully, and then go through the subsequent explanatory points.

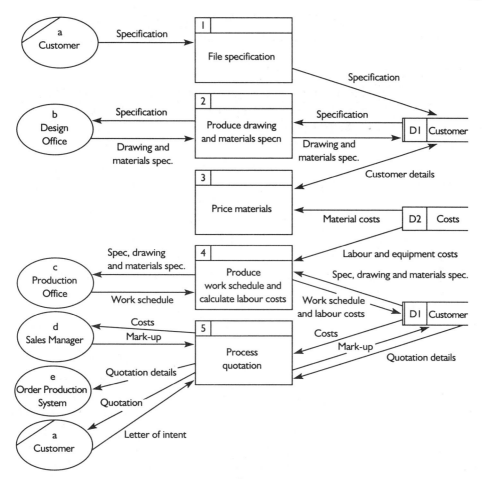

Figure 8.13 Level 1 logical DFD for Marine Construction

In comparing the physical DFDs with the logical equivalent above, note the following points.

1. The seven data stores in the current physical system have been replaced by two logical data stores. D1 is the Customer File and contains details of the specification, the drawing, the materials specification, the work schedule and the overall quotation. D2 is the Costs File and contains all the necessary data for Materials, Labour and Equipment costs. This seemed the most logical way to split the data: D1 is current work and D2 is standing reference data.

2. The Design Office has been removed as an external entity. Its function is still needed to produce the drawing from the specification and decide what materials

are to be used, but the system will then store these details. In a computerized system, one can imagine the use of computer-aided design to produce the drawing which is then linked to the Customer Specification and the Materials Specification.

3. We have assumed that, for the production of quotations, the Materials Office is not logically required. If the Materials Specification produced by the Design Office is accurate, then the production of material costs is logically done by reference to the Costs File.

4. We have assumed that the expertise of the Production Office in producing the Work Schedule is still required and, hence, it is now an external entity. However, if the Work Schedule is accurate, the calculation of labour and equipment costs can be done logically by reference to the Costs File.

5. As mentioned in Chapter 4, the addition of the mark-up to the quotation by the Sales Manager is a subjective process which should not be automated. Hence, the Sales Manager has been removed from the system and shown as an external entity.

8.4 Conclusion

As we said at the beginning of the chapter, some people find logicalization to be difficult and so avoid it like the plague. Others find it intellectually stimulating and very useful. We are strong supporters, even though we agree it can be tricky sometimes. Logicalization basically sorts things out, and is probably the single most important step in the development of a good sound system. It gets you thinking along the right lines and puts the system into its proper perspective. It can be the fundamental turning point between analysis of a current system and design of a worthwhile new one. As explained at the beginning of this chapter, it can also play an important part in the application of a business process re-engineering management strategy; this is increasingly pertinent as companies seek to follow the lead of organizations claiming fundamental efficiency improvements.

Sometimes, the current system is already pretty logical because the physical implementation has been recently and thoroughly thought out and works well. However, particularly if a system has been in place for some time, the process of logicalization can reveal to the systems analyst underlying themes and policies that would normally escape. It is in situations like these where the technique really shows its worth.

Summary

This chapter began by explaining the background to logicalization and introduced you to the related concept of business process re-engineering. We then went through the four steps of logicalization: rationalization of data flows, rationalization of data stores, rationalization of bottom level processes, and re-constructing the DFD.

Further reading

J. Peppard and P. Rowland, *The Essence of Business Process Re-engineering*, Prentice Hall, Hemel Hempstead, 1995.

9

Developing the required system

9.1 Introduction

9.1.1 Learning techniques

This book is mainly about systems analysis *techniques*. We have been introducing you to a range of established and recognized methods of analysing and documenting certain aspects of a system. So, when we wish to describe the processing involved, we use data flow modelling and structured English. When we wish to describe the data, we use data modelling and normalization. There are several techniques which we have not described, that are still necessary for a systems analyst to master: interviewing, project management, handling meetings, and preparing and giving presentations for example are all absolutely essential ingredients for a successful systems analyst. The techniques we have introduced in this book are really those that help describe a system.

We have also treated these techniques largely in isolation. Hence, there are separate chapters on data flow diagramming, entity modelling and the like. In reality, of course, these techniques are frequently done in parallel and they do overlap. For example, in a data flow diagram, you will find data stores. These data stores contain data and the relationships within this data are described using an entity model.

9.1.2 Putting techniques into practice

One of the frequent criticisms of textbooks and courses on system analysis is that, because techniques are often presented in isolation, it is difficult for the reader or the student to link them together and to see how the whole development process works. On other occasions attempts are made to overcome this by having only one large scenario, but this inevitably means that some techniques are demonstrated better than others, depending upon the constraints of the scenario. In this book we are trying to present what we feel to be the best compromise – one scenario that gets revisited as often as is appropriate (the student assessment system), but other examples where these describe a technique better. This chapter again uses the student assessment system as its basis.

We really want to get across the main thrust of how a system is developed up to the point at which we know what the required system is meant to do. In order to do this, we will deliberately leave out a lot of detail and strip the system down to a basic skeleton. This will allow you to see the main *principles* involved without being side-tracked and misled by arguments about detail.

So far, you have been exposed to a number of examples concerning the student assessment system. This has been used to illustrate various techniques such as data flow diagrams, structured English, decision tables and normalization. The separate examples in the different chapters are not really intended to be consistent with one another – we have simply used the system as a good way of illustrating certain concepts. For example, in the chapter on normalization we got really carried away and actually allocated students to tutor groups and tutor groups to tutors. We did this because it was a good way of teaching you about composite or hierarchic keys. The example in the chapter on data flow diagramming did not mention tutor groups at all, and concentrated on the assessment side of things.

You are, by now, used to this system and probably have a good basic understanding of many of its features. You will find that in this chapter the processing side of things is similar to the example in the data flow diagramming chapter (Chapter 4) but that the entity modelling side is deliberately watered-down to aid understanding.

9.2 The existing student assessment system

9.2.1 The scenario

You may remember that the scenario is based on year 2 of a degree course, but the procedures are the same for each year. Recently, our university changed from this system to a modular one and we will show how the changes would be handled using the techniques with which you are now becoming familiar. The description is in Section 4.3.1. We will describe this system using the techniques introduced in this book.

9.2.2 Current physical DFDs

With these we describe the system exactly as it is, warts and all. The processes reflect what is actually done and the participants are the real individuals, groups of people or departments. The data stores are the actual files used. Hence, it is called a physical data flow diagram as it describes exactly what is *physically* going on.

The level 1 and level 2 current physical DFDs for this system taken from Chapter 4 are shown in Figures 9.1–9.4. A detailed description of the procedures involved in Process 3 (Moderate and finalize results) is shown in Figure 9.5 and is taken from Chapter 5 (*Specifying processes*). This description is written using a combination of structured English and decision tables.

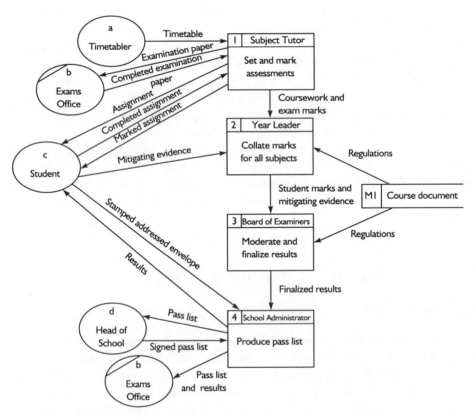

Figure 9.1   Level 1 DFD (current physical) for student assessment system

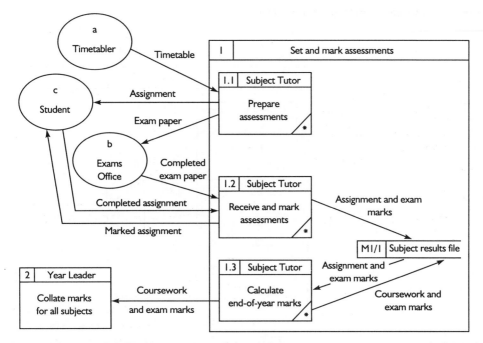

Figure 9.2 Level 2 DFD (current physical) for student assessment system process 1: Set and mark assessments

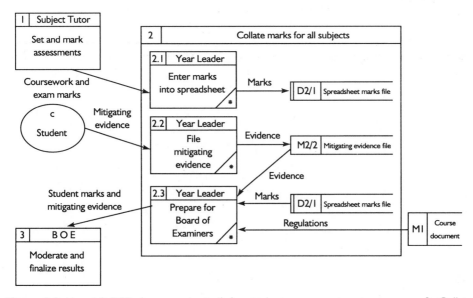

Figure 9.3 Level 2 DFD (current physical) for student assessment system process 2: Collate marks for all subjects

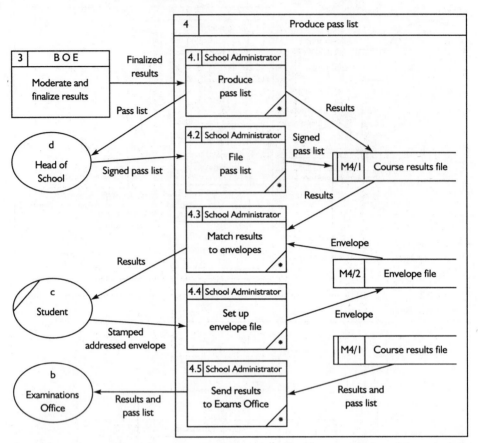

Figure 9.4 Level 2 DFD (current physical) for student assessment system process 4: Produce pass list

Do the following for each student:

Step 1 Determine the number of failed subjects:

A subject is failed if any of the following are asterisked:
- Course-mark
- Exam-mark
- Subject-mark

Step 2 Determine student results:

CASE 1 (Number of subjects failed = 0)
Student has passed the year

CASE 2 (Number of subjects failed = 1 or 2)
For each subject determine the result according to the following decision table:

				E
Course-mark < 40%	Y	N	N	L
Exam-mark < 35%	N	Y	N	S
Subject-mark < 40%	N	N	N	E
Redo coursework	X			X
Resit exam		X		X
Subject passed			X	

CASE 3 (Number of subjects failed > 2)
Determine result according to the following decision table:

Repeat student?	Y	N	N	N
Any Course-mark < 40%	–	Y	N	N
Any Subject-mark < 40%	–	–	Y	N
Leave course	X			
Internal repeat		X	X	
Internal or external repeat				X

Figure 9.5 Process description for process 3: Moderate and finalize results

9.2.3 Current entity model

For the sake of simplicity, we will only consider the entities Course, Subject, Student, and Student Result. We first saw the entity model of the current system in Chapter 8 (Figure 8.5), and it is repeated in Figure 9.6.

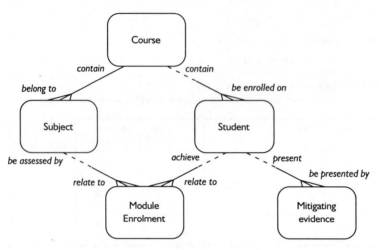

Figure 9.6   Entity model of current system

9.2.4 Current logical DFD

Also in Chapter 8, we saw how the current physical system was stripped of all its physical constraints to reveal the underlying policy behind the system. The level 1 logical DFD for the system, first seen in Figure 8.8, is shown again in Figure 9.7.

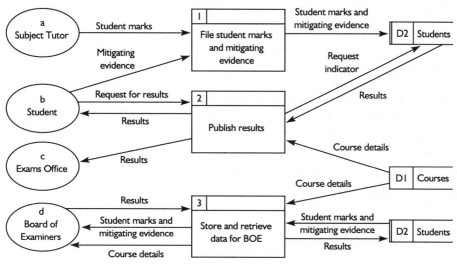

Figure 9.7   Level 1 logical DFD of the current student assessment system

9.3 The requirements of the new student assessment system

Changing from the existing system to a modular one is a huge endeavour. We will simply describe some of the major changes involved.

1. In the existing system, a course contains a number of subjects in each year, and each subject only belongs to one course. In the modular system this is totally changed. A subject is now called a Module, each module being appropriate to a particular level of study. The levels are 1, 2 and 3 which are equivalent to Years 1, 2 and Final Year in the existing system. However, a Module can be part of several Courses. So, students from several courses could all be studying the same module. A Course is, hence, made up from a number of Modules, some of which are *core* (or compulsory) for a course and some of which may be *optional*.

2. Instead of one Board of Examiners for a course, there will now be two. Each module will have a Board which will examine the results for each module. When all the Module Boards are complete, each Course will have a Board which will look at the complete set of module results for each student and decide on progression. The rules and regulations for this Course Board are too complicated to describe here.

3. The computer system will hold full details of Students, Courses, Modules and Module Enrolments. Details of members of staff will not be held in this computer system. Module leaders and course leaders will be held in a parallel manual system. In the current system, the Course and Subject details are held in a Course

document, which describes the course in detail, the subjects which make it up and the regulations which apply to the course. In the new system, the relationships between Course and Module must be stored in the computer to allow students to study the correct modules on their chosen course.

4. The Year Leader does not appear in the new system. It is the responsibility of the module leader to provide student results to the School Administrator for entry into the computer system before the Module Boards. Any changes to the results arising from the Board will be entered by the School Administrator before the Course Board.

The above is a limited set of requirements, but they all impact upon either the entity model or data flow diagrams or both.

9.4 The required system

9.4.1 The required entity model

The only really major change to the current entity model is due to the change in nature of a Subject. It is now called a Module, and its relationship to a Course is now many-to-many instead of one-to-many. Normalization of data also throws up two new entities called Result and Module Type (which are really look-up tables – refer to Chapter 7 on normalization, where these two entities are described in more detail). Hence, the required entity model is shown in Figure 9.8.

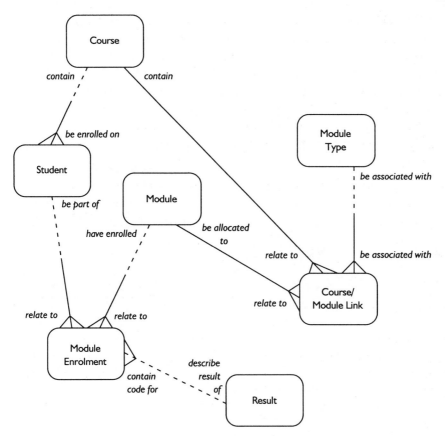

Figure 9.8 Entity model for required student assessment system

9.4.2 The required DFD

Requirements 2 and 4 in Section 9.3 force changes to the data flow diagram. A level 1 required data flow diagram is shown in Figure 9.9.

You can see that this diagram shows the person or persons interacting with the system. In this case, the only person entering data is the School Adminstrator who will actually have a number of clerks to help. Any data transferred between external entities, which are necessary to the functioning of the system, are also shown using dotted lines and this helps in the design of clerical procedures later on in the system development.

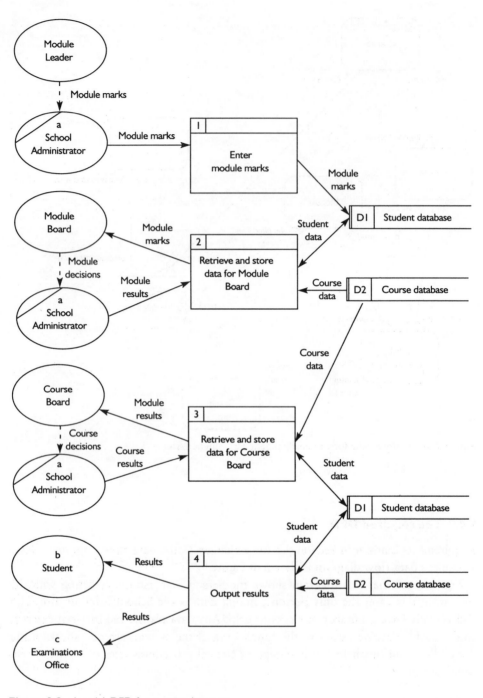

Figure 9.9 Level I DFD for required system

9.5 What is missing?

9.5.1 No maintenance

The answer to the above question is: *a great deal!* You may have thought that this chapter has been straightforward enough, but we have deliberately missed out several important things simply to show the general direction in which systems analysis proceeds.

If the system modelled in the required data flow diagram were implemented as it stands, the system would soon fall flat on its face. Have you noticed, for instance, that there is *no maintenance*. How does a student get on to the system in the first place, where do courses come from and where do we allocate modules to courses? What happens when a student changes address or when a module becomes defunct? All of these considerations are looked upon as standard *maintenance* questions which any self-respecting systems analyst usually considers as a matter of course.

This will be explored more fully in the next chapter when we look at such things as entity life histories and (briefly) state transition diagrams, which make sure that we have thought of everything. In actual fact, the system will be *maintained* by the School Administrator who will enter new students, courses and modules into the system.

When starting out in systems analysis, you will have to watch out for such things. During your systems investigation it is obvious that you will be exposed to the day-to-day operations and may not witness or be told about the procedures that are only done occasionally. In our example, new courses will only appear once every two years or so, and you must get into the habit of questioning how every entity begins its life and meets its end. As already mentioned, the next chapter includes techniques which make sure you do this, and so the final version of the required data flow diagram is left until then.

9.5.2 No alternatives

Our *required* system seems to have just come together of its own accord. In practice, there may be several ways of implementing requirements and, usually, several options are considered that implement the requirements in different ways and to different extents. Some of these will be cheaper than others and cost will be a prime consideration for the user.

In addition to these different approaches to functionality, there will be different approaches to hardware configuration. Some options may involve a stand-alone machine, others a network configuration and others a central processor linked to users through terminals. In practice, however, most computer systems are designed for computer configurations that already exist. We have really looked at functional requirements.

The implementation of those requirements is not the subject of systems analysis but the province of systems design, which is beyond the scope of this book.

Summary

This chapter began by drawing together most of the techniques taught in this book. It looked at the student assessment case study and brought together all the diagrams drawn up to this point. It then introduced you to some requirements for this case study and showed how these could be implemented by changes to the entity model and data flow diagrams. It finished by raising the question of completeness.

Further reading

G. Cutts, *Structured Systems Analysis and Design Methodology*, 2nd edn, Chapter 5, Alfred Waller, Henley-on-Thames, 1991.

10

The effect of time

So far in this book we have looked at two main aspects of a system – processing and data. The processing view will be the foundation of the computer programs and the data view will be the basis of the computer files or databases. They interact to a great extent because processing affects data by reading it, updating it or deleting it. These two views are extremely important and fundamental to the development of a system, but do not give the complete picture. What is missing is the concept of time.

Time considerations can be thought of as the glue which holds the system together. By considering this extra dimension, we can control the sequence of processes and make sure that a system does not do anything that it should not do at a particular point. The techniques involved also force us to consider the complete life of a system and its constituent parts, and therefore, help considerably in ensuring that the system is as complete as possible.

In methods like SSADM the technique which models time (strictly speaking it models *events* and we consider this in Section 10.5) is so fundamental that it is used as the major plank for developing process specifications in preference to the DFDs, which are considered too imprecise to be of much further use.

The main part of this chapter is concerned with the processing aspects of a system, but we begin by considering how time can affect the data model.

10.2 Time and the data model

We will tackle this topic by revisiting the description of a vehicle breakdown and rescue system which we first met in Chapter 6.

Each engineer is allocated one van (which is driven up to a certain mileage and then replaced). Each member has only one address but perhaps many vehicles. Each visit is to deal with only one vehicle. A member can be visited more than once on any given date, and there may be many visits to a member on different dates. A member may only be covered for some of the vehicles they own and not for others.

When we looked at this we decided that Engineer and Van (among others) were probably entities in the system. Let us look at the relationship between these two entities. We will assume that one Engineer is allocated one Van and that the Van belongs to only one Engineer and is not shared. The Engineers may even be allowed to keep their vans at their houses overnight. The system is only required to keep track of existing Engineers and their current Vans. This is obviously a one-to-one relationship which can be expressed as follows. One Engineer *must* be allocated *only one* Van and one Van *may* be allocated to *only one* Engineer.

By using the word *may* in the second half of the sentence we have allowed for spare Vans which are only used if an allocated Van breaks down. A diagrammatic representation of the relationship is shown in Figure 10.1.

Figure 10.1   A representation of relationship between Engineer and Van

However, what if we wanted to keep a historical record of Engineers and their Vans? Vans will eventually become unreliable and need to be replaced. They can also become involved in accidents. The managers of the company might well wish to check which Engineers looked after their Vans reasonably and also look at the history of a particular Van.

Simply by introducing *history* into the system, we make the data model more complex. The relationship between Engineer and Van now becomes many-to-many as an Engineer can be allocated more than one Van over the period of their employment and a Van can be allocated to more than one Engineer over its lifespan.

The data model now changes quite dramatically and, if we wish to differentiate between current and previous allocations, is represented by Figure 10.2.

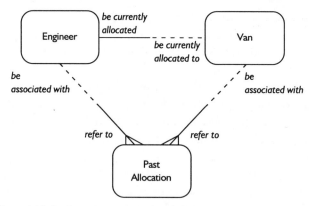

Figure 10.2 Introducing *history* into the relationship

This situation happens frequently. For example, in a library system, a Book can only be on loan to one Borrower at a time and this *current loan* relationship is one-to-one. However, the library may well wish to keep records of loans once the books have been returned for statistical purposes. For example, they may wish to find out the most popular and least popular books. This makes the relationship between Book and Borrower many-to-many in the same way as Engineer and Van. It is well worth watching out for this when investigating a system as it is a common feature of several systems.

10.3 Time and the DFD

It might be worth your while having a quick look back at Chapters 3 and 4 – the ones on data flow diagrams (DFDs). DFDs can cause a lot of trouble because their purpose is often misinterpreted. We commonly find that students (and sometimes practising systems analysts) try to impose time sequencing onto a DFD when it is really not one of its purposes. Before DFDs became such a popular and powerful technique, system processes were often shown using various forms of *flowchart*. Flowcharts are often taught in schools as part of mathematics or computer studies courses and they *do* show the sequencing of operations. Because DFDs and flowcharts can *look* so similar and because a lot of people meet flowcharts before DFDs, they often confuse the two and it is often hard to adapt to the principles of the DFD.

A good example of this occurred in Chapter 4 when we looked at the processes involved in producing quotations for a company called Marine Construction. You may remember that we started off by following a form called a BQ1 around the system in a sequential manner and discovered that it started off in the Sales Office, went round a couple of departments and then returned to the Sales Office. We drew this sequential set of operations as a level 1 DFD, and then *re-drew* it by grouping together all the operations for one department and making each department one process box on the DFD.

A DFD does not really consider time at all, and is not intended to. It simply shows the data flowing into and out from a system, where the data comes from and where it goes to, what processes act on the data flows and which data stores are affected by these processes. It does not address the sequencing of the processes and several mistakes are made when people assume that it does.

Of course, in reality, some processes cannot start before other processes have finished. Some processes will only start if a certain set of conditions have been satisfied in other processes. The only circumstance where a DFD shows this is when one process sends data directly to another, rather than first sending it elsewhere.

It is time to introduce *events*.

10.4 Events

10.4.1 What is an event?

An event is something that happens in the real world that changes one or more of the entities in the system under consideration. It is the trigger which brings one or more of the processes in the DFDs into action.

This is the secret behind the sequencing of operations. Although it is the *process* that updates an entity, it is the *event* which triggers this process. Hence, the control of processes is really about the ways in which events affect the system.

10.4.2 Finding events in DFDs

It is very useful to think of an event as just something that happens and this *something* has an effect on one or more entities in the system. As an event *always* triggers a process, there is a strong link between events and DFDs. The most obvious events are obtained by looking at the data flows on a DFD. We will demonstrate this by referring again to the level 1 required DFD for the student record system which we first met in Chapter 9 (see Figure 10.3).

10.4.3 Types of event

Externally generated events

Process 1 is called Enter module marks and is performed by the School Administrator. The event which triggers this process is the arrival of the module marks from the

Module Leader: this is the thing which happens which gets the School Administrator to enter the marks. This event would be probably described as *Receipt of module marks* or something similar. This is an example of an *externally generated* event and is shown as a data flow across the system boundary.

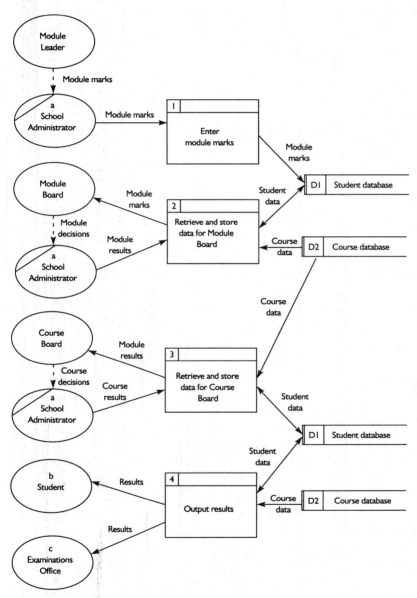

Figure 10.3 A level I DFD for required system

Internally recognized events

This occurs when something happens within the system which causes a subsequent event to occur. For example, within process 2 (Retrieve and store data for Module Board), students who fail a module will be highlighted. This would be shown in a level 2 DFD and the associated process descriptions. Recognizing a *fail* is an event which will cause that student's module record to be updated. This is an *internally recognized* event.

Time-based events

This occurs when a process is triggered simply because a particular time has been reached. An example might be the automatic deletion of records that have been inactive for over a year. The event is the arrival of a particular time. This is a *time-based* event.

10.5 Entity Life Histories (ELHs)

10.5.1 What is an ELH?

An Entity Life History (ELH) is a diagram which looks at all of the possible events that can affect an entity. Within SSADM these diagrams are absolutely crucial as they form the basis for process specification using Jackson-type structures (see Chapter 1, Section 1.1.3) to show the sequence in which these events can occur. In SSADM, this transition from ELHs and entity models through an effect correspondence diagram to a Jackson program structure is complete, concise and intellectually beautiful. However, it does pre-judge that you are going to design your processes using Jackson structures, and this is far from true in most system development nowadays. Also, we have found that ELHs are sometimes difficult to get right when there are several events that can affect an entity and the sequencing requirements are a little complex. As a result, we are going to show you a slightly watered down version of ELHs which misses out some of the complexities that occur. We will also introduce you to a simple home grown procedure that some students have found helpful in drawing ELHs.

Whilst ELHs are widespread within organizations and university/college courses and most of the remainder of this chapter is subsequently devoted to them, there are other techniques which serve the same purpose. We will introduce you to one of these at the end of the chapter.

10.5.2 Drawing an ELH

Figure 10.4 shows the entity model for the required student record system which we last discussed in Chapter 9.

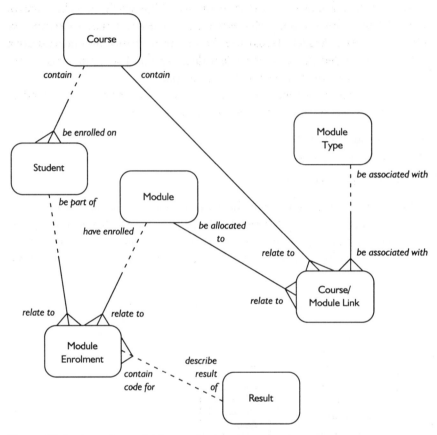

Figure 10.4   An entity model for required student record system

The point to note is that each entity in the system has a life history, so in this system there should be seven ELHs, i.e. one for each of the entities Student, Course, Module, Module Type, Course/Module Link, Module Enrolment and Result. Let us look at the life history of the entity Student.

Creation and deletion events

These should always be the first events to be considered when drawing an ELH. What causes a Student record to be placed on the system in the first place? When students arrive, they are required to register and this event triggers the creation of a Student record on the database. Hence the creation event is Student Registration.

What causes a Student record to be deleted from the system? We will assume that a Student record is kept on the system until a year after they have left the university. Their records are then removed to another Archive File which, for the sake of simplicity, is part of another system. Hence the deletion event is time-based and we will call it One Year After Student Departure. This event will obviously depend upon the system having recorded the date of student departure and so cannot take place until the previous event Student Departure has taken place.

We, hence, have a strict sequence of events. For every occurrence of the Student entity, the above three events *must* occur in the following sequence.

Student Registration followed by

Student Departure followed by

One Year After Student Departure.

The second event cannot occur without the first event having taken place and the third event cannot occur without the second. In ELH notation this is drawn as in Figure 10.5. This is a *sequence* construct. The sequence progresses from left to right. The name of the entity is always shown in a rectangular box at the top of the diagram.

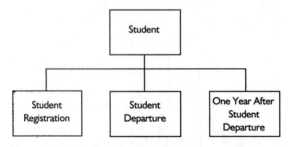

Figure 10.5   An ELH for Student entity

Mid-life events

What can happen to a Student between arriving and leaving? Obviously all sorts of things, but we are only interested in events which change the entity. The most common occurrence, which happens to all entities in all systems, is an *amendment* or change to one of the data items in the Student record. For example, a Student might change address or there might have been a mistake when the Student details were first entered. We will assume that these amendments or changes can only take place between Student Registration and Student Departure. Also, you will realize that the event Student Amendment can take place more than once for a particular Student. It is, hence, an iterative event. Inclusion of this event changes the ELH as in Figure 10.6.

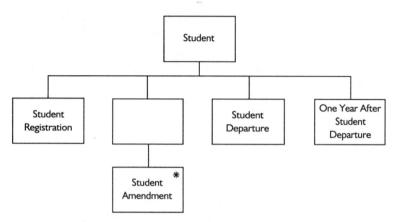

Figure 10.6 An ELH for Student entity

Notice the asterisk in the top right hand corner of the new event which indicates an iteration. An iteration can occur zero, one or many times, and so this allows for there being no amendments to a particular Student record throughout its life. Also note that the new event is a level below the other sequenced events with a *dummy* box above it. This is because you are not allowed to mix different constructs at the same level in an ELH.

What else can happen to a Student in their life? They will enrol on modules. However, does enrolment on a module affect the Student entity? If you look at the entity model, enrolment on a module will create a new entity Module Enrolment which is linked to the entity Student.

In a relational data base there is no processing as such which forms this link – it is simply a relationship between keys. Nevertheless, it is normal practice to show the formation of this link on the ELHs of both the entities involved in the link, as in other database management systems some processing takes place in establishing the link.

Hence, we have another event called Module Enrolment which will happen several times and is, therefore, an iteration. However, if we now draw the ELH as in Figure 10.7, we cause problems.

This solution is wrong as it implies that all of the Module Enrolments have to be done before all of the Student Amendments which is obviously incorrect. The two events are interspersed and can occur in parallel with each other.

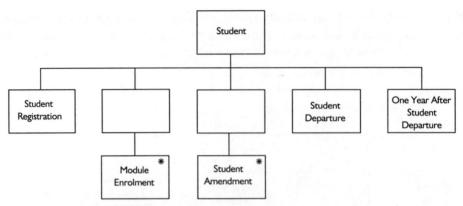

Figure 10.7   An ELH for Student entity, including Module Enrolment event

Some texts actually describe a special construct for parallel events, but there is an alternative which uses more *standard* constructs and we prefer it because we feel it keeps things simple. This sort of situation happens in several systems and we would show it as in Figure 10.8.

The circles in the top right hand corner of the middle boxes are *selection* symbols. Basically, the diagram is saying that after Student Registration, there is an iteration,

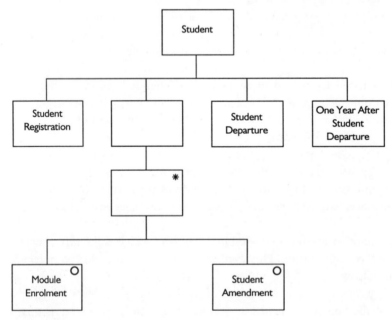

Figure 10.8   An ELH for Student entity including Module Enrolment event, utilizing selection

each occurrence of which is *either* a Student Amendment *or* a Module Enrolment. These diagrams get very complex very quickly. Students are allowed to withdraw from Modules and we would have to show Module Withdrawal as a separate event as this removes the link between Student and Module Enrolment.

In addition, we may wish to update the Student record differently depending upon the nature of Student Departure. If a Student were to leave the university prematurely as opposed to leaving when the course was completed, the processing involved may well be different. The event Student Departure now becomes qualified into two sub-events as follows.

Student Departure (Premature)

Student Departure (Course Completed)

The items in brackets are called *effect qualifiers*. The final ELH for the Student entity is shown in Figure 10.9. Included are two new events. Yearly Course Result which updates the Student's course status decided at the Course Board, and Course Completed which occurs after the Final Course Board for a Student. The fact that a Student cannot complete their course until they have gained a certain number of credits is not governed by this ELH. The Course Board decides whether a Student qualifies for an Award after looking at the profile of each Student.

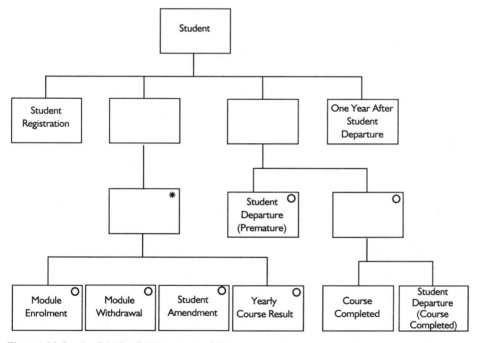

Figure 10.9 An ELH for Student entity, final version

The ELH for the entity Module Enrolment would be constructed in a similar fashion, and is shown in Figure 10.10. Note the inclusion of a *null* box, which indicates that a module withdrawal may not happen

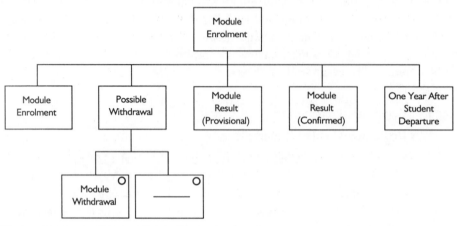

Figure 10.10 An ELH for Module Enrolment entity

10.5.3 The entity/event matrix

Example incorporating Student and Module Enrolment entities

The entity/event matrix is a very useful grid which is often constructed before the ELHs are drawn. We have developed our own extension of this approach, which many students have found assists greatly in the creation of a correctly drawn ELH. This is described fully in the section *Creating an ELH by further analysis of the entity/event matrix*.

A partially completed matrix for our system is shown in Figure 10.11 – showing the events for the two entities which have already been discussed. The entries C, M and D stand for create, modify and delete respectively and are known as *effects*.

Event \ Entity	Student	Module Enrlmt	Course	Module	Course/ Module	Result	Module Type
Student Registration	C						
Student Departure (Premature)	M						
Student Departure (Course Cmplt)	M						
One Year After Student Departure	D	D					
Student Amendment	M						
Module Enrolment	M	C					
Module Withdrawal	M	M					
Module Result (Provisional)		M					
Module Result (Confirmed)		M					
Course Completed	M						
Yearly Course Result	M						

Figure 10.11 Partially completed entity/event matrix showing Student and Module Enrolment entities

This matrix is very useful. First, it acts as a check that every entity has a create and delete event. You may remember that our required DFD did not consider the processing associated with these events. Secondly, it makes you think very carefully about all the things that can happen to a particular entity. This entity/event approach is crucial because thinking in this way ensures that as much of the required processing as possible is considered. It provides an extra perspective to the systems analysis that has so far been missing and, in our view, this is the main benefit of the technique – it is an aid to ensuring the analysis is complete. Thirdly, it ensures that all the entities which are affected by one event are considered together. You will notice that a number of the events in the matrix affect both of the entities Student and Module Enrolment.

The columns of the matrix form the basis of the ELHs and the rows form the basis of an SSADM diagramming technique called *Effect Correspondence Diagrams* (ECDs) which eventually lead to Jackson process structures (Section 1.1.3). However, this book does not consider these latter techniques and interested readers should refer to SSADM textbooks – a favourite of ours is mentioned at the end of the chapter.

Creating an ELH by further analysis of the entity/event matrix

Some students take quite easily to the concepts of entity life histories and how to draw them. If you are not one of these, do not despair. Instead, read on. In teaching ELH diagramming we have developed our own simple extension of the above approach, which many students have found helpful. It uses further analysis of the entity/event matrix to first create the variety of constructs which it describes, and then put these constructs together to create the final diagram. We have found that it provides a fairly foolproof means of coming up with a practical ELH. Before we leave entity/event matrices we will, therefore, give an example of how this approach can be applied. To do so, we will consider the following scenario which describes a simple hotel booking system.

A reservation request is received and a reservation is then entered into the system. However, a reservation is not always made – guests sometimes turn up in the hope of finding a free room. In some cases, a deposit is received after the reservation has been made and this is entered into the system. On the day a guest is to check in, a room is allocated to the reservation. When the guest arrives the reservation becomes a booking or, if a reservation has not been made, a booking is created. Chargeable items are entered into the system as and when they arise and a running total is kept on the Reservation/Booking entity. When the guest departs an invoice is produced. At the end of each month paid bookings are removed to the Booking History file.

Before reading further you may like to go over the above description carefully again, and try to produce an ELH for the entity Reservation/Booking based upon what you have seen so far, i.e. either by attempting to draw an ELH directly from the description, or by first creating an entity/event matrix. To keep things simple, ignore the possibility of a Reservation/Booking being cancelled or amended.

The ELH in Figure 10.12 is a typical answer. Whether or not you have had a go at drawing your own, you should check Figure 10.12 against the scenario. You should be able to confirm that it meets all the requirements of the scenario, and is a perfectly proper solution.

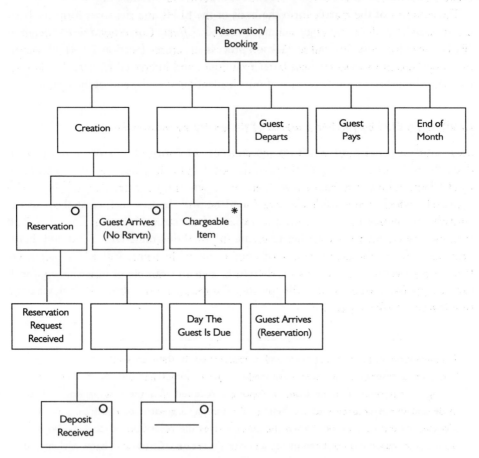

Figure 10.12 Completed ELH for Reservation/Booking (version 1)

One obvious feature however is the very complicated Creation stage. This makes the system look rather *front heavy* and it is possible to produce a simpler version using a methodical approach rather than the semi-intuitive one used so far. This time we will carefully decide upon the best constructs by using the entity/event matrix to the full.

Before we do so, however, it is time to mention an added refinement: the use of *quits* and *resumes*. These allow you to skip events which are unnecessary under certain conditions. They are often frowned upon by purists but can lead to a simpler, more practical solution. For those who have experience of an appropriate programming language, it is helpful to think of these in terms of *by-passing a sub-routine*.

As stated, we will begin by creating the entity/event matrix, but this time we will add selection (either this event or that one) and iteration (an event which can happen repeatedly) notations to the right of each appropriate create, modify or delete effect. Those without either of these *special* notations must by default be a simple sequence. By using *quits* and *resumes* we will also add any instances where, following a certain action, any other events may be *skipped*. These are always numbered. Q1 leads to R1, Q2 to R2 etc. If there is a *quit*, there must of course be a corresponding *resume*. In the example we are considering, there is only one instance of a Q–R. This may all sound somewhat confusing at present, but we will go through the process step by step and everything should then become clear.

Re-read the scenario and compare it with the entity/event matrix in Figure 10.13, which you will see includes (to the right of some of the C/M/D effects):

* *mini* versions of the ELH select, iteration and null notations introduced in the subsection *Mid-life events*;

* a quit and resume as described above.

Event \ Entity	Resrvtn/ Booking
Reservation Request Received	C $^{\circ}$
Deposit Received	M $^{\circ -}$
Day Arrives When Guest Is Due	M
Guest Arrives (Reservation)	M
Guest Arrives (No Reservation)	C $^{\circ}$ (Q1)
Chargeable Item Arises	M * (R1)
Guest Departs	M
Guest Pays	M
End of Month	D

Figure 10.13   Completed ELH for Reservation/Booking (version 1)

To clarify things further, we will now show step-by-step how the above was derived. Having listed the *events*, the process which leads to the allocation of the *effects* and *ELH notations* is fairly straightforward, and is in three stages.

1. *Identify and analyse creation event(s)*. A sensible interpretation of the scenario is that there is a choice of *two* events which can do this. These are Reservation Request Received, or Guest Arrives without a Reservation. A 'C' is therefore entered alongside each of these, and '°' added to indicate selection. It is also noted that if Guest Arrives without a Reservation is the event which occurs, then other events are not applicable (i.e. Deposit Received, Day Arrives when Guest is Due, Guest Arrives with Reservation). A 'Q' is therefore shown alongside the Guest Arrives without a Reservation event. We now need to identify the next event that could possibly take place after the skipped ones are passed over. It is obvious that this is Chargeable Item Arises, and so 'R1' is entered to indicate where the resume occurs.

2. *Identify and analyse deletion event(s)*. It is obvious from the scenario that this occurs only with the End Of Month event. A 'D' is therefore entered alongside this. No alternative event is involved, so no further notation is entered.

3. *Identify and analyse modification event(s)*. Having identified all events appropriate to creation and deletion, all other events must by default be modification ones – so an 'M' is placed alongside these. Taking each in turn, we now use the scenario to identify whether any are *selected* ones. This can either be because some *other* event may alternatively take place (as happened with the create effect), or because *no* event may alternatively take place, i.e. an alternate *null* as introduced at the end of the section *Mid-life events*. In this case we see that the Deposit Received event may or may not occur, so '°-' is entered beside the M. A little more analysis of the scenario establishes that there are no further *select* events.

We therefore turn to the final ELH notation, i.e. that of *iteration*. This was ignored when we were considering creates and deletes, because each of these can of course only happen once. But does the scenario describe any modify events which can take place more than once during the life of the entity? We see that there is one, i.e. Chargeable Item Arises. An asterisk * is therefore entered alongside this one.

With the matrix thus annotated as described, it is time to draw the identified non-sequence constructs, as shown in Figure 10.14.

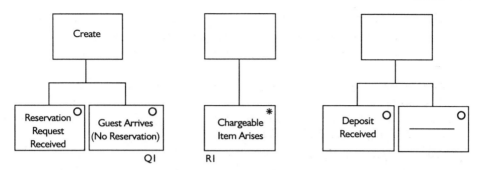

Figure 10.14 Reservation/booking ELH constructs for Create, Chargeable Item Arises and Deposit Received

Each of these complete constructs will be in some sort of sequence within the life of the Reservation/Booking, as will all the remaining events on the matrix. It is now simply a case of putting them together.

The *creation* obviously comes first, and the End of Month event represents the delete, which comes last (see Figure 10.15).

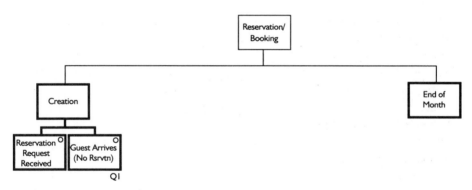

Figure 10.15 Reservation/booking ELH stage 1

We have said that every other construct comes in between, in sequence – so we now need to add these. But, creation consists of two possible events here. Which do we begin with in order to identify the subsequent event? It should be fairly evident that we choose the one which has no quit, i.e. Reservation Request Received, because if it has no quit the next possible event *has* to follow it. We note from the scenario that the next possible event to this would be Deposit Received. We have a pre-drawn construct with Deposit Received within it, so we simply add this whole construct to the sequence (see Figure 10.16).

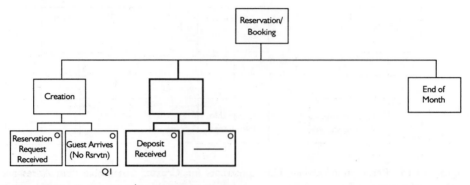

Figure 10.16   Reservation/Booking ELH stage 2

We then do the same to all other events which happen sequentially following the reservation request. If we have a pre-drawn construct, we include it; if not, we simply enter the event in a box of its own.

First, two events without a pre-drawn construct (Figure 10.17) are followed by the next pre-drawn one (Figure 10.18) and then the last two, which again are not pre-drawn and are therefore simply shown in single boxes (Figure 10.19).

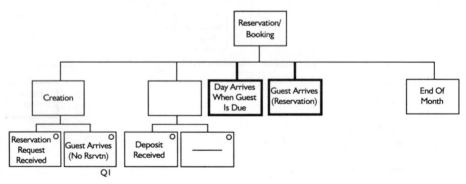

Figure 10.17   Reservation/Booking ELH stage 3

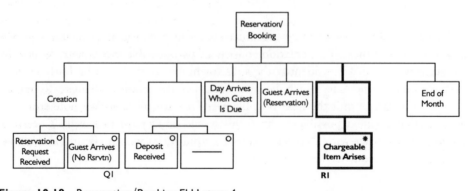

Figure 10.18   Reservation/Booking ELH stage 4

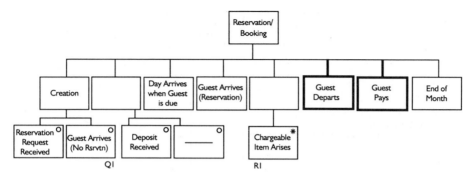

Figure 10.19 Completed ELH for Reservation/Booking (version 2)

It can be seen that by blindly following our annotated entity/event matrix together with the pre-drawn constructs where appropriate, our quit–resume feature has automatically been taken care of, i.e. if the event Guest Arrives (No Reservation) takes place, Q1 jumps directly to R1 at Chargeable Item Arises.

Even a quick comparison with version 1 of the ELH (Figure 10.12) shows that we have created a diagram with a far simpler creation stage – and we have done so using a step-by-step approach that is probably more reliable than the partially intuitive one. Many texts seem to expect an ELH to be put together in some intuitive way. Perhaps with experience it is possible to do so, but we hope that at least for the present the above approach will help you create diagrams that are reliable and practical.

10.5.4 The process/event matrix

This matrix maps events to DFD processes. Each event *must* trigger a process or processes and the main benefit of this matrix is that it sometimes traps missing processes. A sample matrix is shown in Figure 10.20 for our student record system. The matrix contains only the events we have met so far, i.e. the ones which affect the entities Student and Module Enrolment.

The first thing to note is that the process Output Results does not have an associated event. This is because the process does not actually update anything, but simply retrieves data and prints it out. However, the most striking feature of this matrix is that all of the events that trigger simple maintenance processing do not have a process present on the DFD.

Please note that this example is rather extreme and it is very unlikely that such a situation would have been allowed to go un-noticed up to this point. Nevertheless, it is important to note that unless you undertake some event modelling, it is possible for processes to be missed. Even so, there is no guarantee that construction of ELHs will discover everything.

Event / Process	Enter module marks	Retrieve and store data for Module Board	Retrieve and store data for Course Board	Output results	No process present for this event
Student Registration					X
Student Departure (Premature)					X
Student Depature (Course Complt)					X
One Year After Student Departure					X
Student Amendment					X
Module Enrolment					X
Module Withdrawal					X
Module Result (Provisional)	X				
Module Result (Confirmed)		X			
Course Completed			X		
Yearly Course Result			X		

Figure 10.20 Partially completed process/event matrix showing events which affect Student and Module Enrolment entities

If the fact finding and general observation is not thorough enough, certain *events* may well be missed. A revised level 1 DFD of the required system incorporating missing maintenance functions is now shown in Figure 10.21, and a level 2 DFD for the maintenance functions is shown in Figure 10.22.

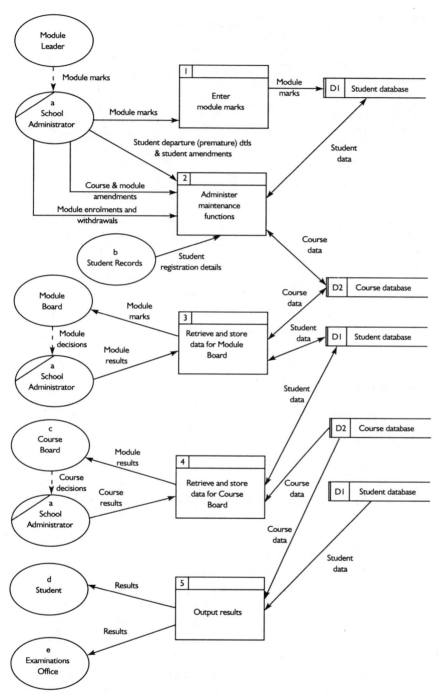

Figure 10.21 Revised level 1 DFD of the required system incorporating missing maintenance functions

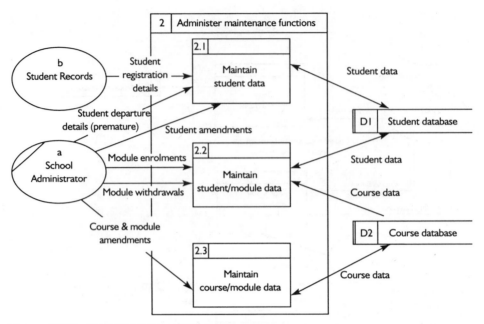

Figure 10.22 Level 2 DFD for maintenance functions

10.5.5 State indicators and the control of processes

ELHs provide a framework which shows the systems analyst in which sequence events should be allowed to affect an entity. How do we make sure that the processing triggered by an event happens at the right time and does not take place *illegally*? For example, in the Student entity, we have to make sure that the event One year after Student Departure takes place after the event Student Departure has taken place. How do we prevent a Student record being deleted before a Student leaves? One very attractive and simple way of doing this is to have a *state indicator* associated with each event on an ELH. A state indicator is simply an extra data item in the entity which changes to a unique value after each event. So, after the create event Student Registration, the Student state indicator would be set to 1. Each subsequent event would then change it to a new value. State indicators are often shown on the ELH as in Figure 10.23. The number(s) before the '/' symbol are the allowable values of the state indicator before the event can take place. The number after the '/' is the value to which the state indicator is set after the processing triggered by the event has taken place.

It is easy to see that this can be used as an effective means to stop processing taking place out of sequence. A simple check of the state indicator at the start of a

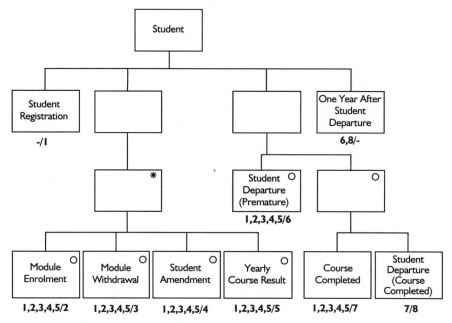

Figure 10.23   An ELH for Student entity, showing state indicators

process would make sure that its value would allow the process to continue. If the state indicator was not one of the allowable values, an error message would be displayed and the process abandoned.

State indicators can enforce a sequence that is difficult to show using the Jackson structures, and you often come across ELHs where the state indicators show the correct sequencing, whereas the ELH structure is either incorrect or misleading.

10.6 State transition diagrams

Another way of showing the same principles as the ELH is a technique called the state transition diagram. There are variations on the way these diagrams are drawn but our favourite representation is the so-called *fence diagram*. A fence diagram for the life of the Student entity is shown in Figure 10.24.

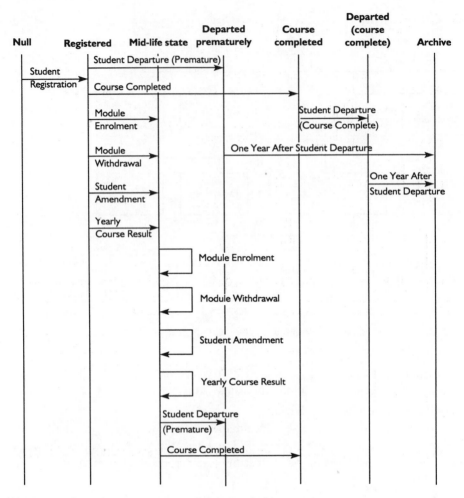

Figure 10.24   A fence diagram for the life of the Student entity

You will notice in this diagram that *states* are shown as *vertical* lines, joined by the occurrence of *events* which are labelled *horizontal* lines. We have not distinguished between the mid-life states produced by the four events Module Enrolment, Module Withdrawal, Student Amendment and Yearly Course Result. This is because it is of little or no use to the system to know which of these transactions was the last to affect the Student entity.

This sort of diagram provides greater flexibility than an ELH, as you can really go from any state to any other state quite easily. In an ELH it is sometimes quite difficult, often requiring the liberal use of quits and resumes.

10.7 Conclusion

Consideration of data and processing alone in the development of a system is not enough. It is easy to miss things out, particularly processing which occurs on an infrequent basis. By considering all the changes that can occur to each entity over the period of its life, we often find additional functions which were missed the first time around. Construction of ELHs or state transition diagrams adds completeness to the systems analysis and provides an extra important view which can then be taken into the design phase.

Summary

This chapter began by looking at how time can affect the data model and then went on to introduce the concept of events. Different types of events were described and you were introduced to a diagram called an entity life history (ELH) which looks at the ways events affect an entity. Through an example, the three constructs of sequence, selection and iteration were described. The entity/event matrix was introduced as a valuable aid in the construction of an ELH, and the process/event matrix was mentioned as a valuable way of spotting missing processes. The chapter ended with a description of state indicators and state transition diagrams.

Further reading

M. Goodland and C. Slater, *SSADM Version 4: A Practical Approach*, McGraw-Hill, London, 1995.

11

The systems analysis environment

11.1 The role of the systems analyst

Historically, many people have become systems analysts after working in the 'harder' end of the computing profession – programming, testing, debugging. Business areas which were 'computerized' were largely the simpler ones and involved relatively unsophisticated users, often with little conceptual understanding of why things happened a certain way – they were simply paid to fill in this form, pass it to that person, etc. It was therefore more realistic to train computer people to understand the business system rather than train users to understand the computer technology. With the automation of ever more complex areas, and the general increase in computer literacy, the trend has now reversed with an increasing number of analysts never having been employed as programmers. Some were previously so-called 'intelligent users' (a term with dubious implications, but often used!), whilst an increasing number have gained a computing qualification at university and have found systems analysis to be their chosen area of the profession. You may someday find yourself among this latter group.

Although some people are expected to cover both functions, as 'analyst programmers', the roles usually require very different personal qualities. For the programmer, interpersonal relationships are often not a primary requirement – the job tends to be a more lonely one. Its frustrations are primarily found in the area of getting a computer system to work, but the bright side is that the programmer who has just found and sorted out a bug is usually allowed to look upon it as a moment of individual success.

The systems analyst often has to be able to work in very different circumstances. Analysis can typically involve much discussion and negotiation and can thus depend heavily upon interpersonal relationships – with other analysts and also users who can easily prove hostile. There is nothing definite about analysis – and the decision to consider a design 'complete' is often dictated by deadline rather than the satisfaction of *knowing* that it is! In the most complicated systems, so many compromises may be necessary that no one is completely happy with the result, and individual users may easily be so rankled by their own concessions that they fail to recognize what the analyst has achieved in gaining any agreement at all.

You still want to be a systems analyst? Good for you! For, despite the above, it can be an extremely satisfying profession. To make it so, however, you need to become better than anyone else at being clear as to what the objectives of a situation are. You need to able to see the wood among the trees. You need to be the one to pull a project together, drive it along. No one else will! Here's how you do it.

11.2 Establishing what you have to do

11.2.1 The theory of *Management By Objectives* (MBO)

This book has introduced a range of techniques designed to equip you as a systems analyst for solving a wide range of business and information system problems. You will not need to be conversant only with analysis techniques, however. Whilst familiarity with these will certainly equip you for solving quite complex problems, modern business demands will mean that you will inevitably also be expected to work to a tight deadline. This means that you must be able to define and work to clearly identified objectives with a minimum of wasted time and effort, and commonly in co-operation with others as members of a team. Key decisions that need to be made at the commencement of a project concern the balance which it is necessary to strike between the degree of thoroughness and the time available. Is the project one in which extremely high quality and thoroughness are the prime considerations? Many set out to be, only to be hurriedly finished off as time and/or cost considerations begin to apply increasing pressure to have the system installed as quickly as possible. Clarification at the outset as to the real objectives, results in a project where everyone is clear as to what is expected and one which has far more chance of remaining under control until the end. This chapter will show you how to be objectives driven, and how to use this approach to work as an effective team member and contribute to the overall management of a project. It all begins with the application of *Management By Objectives* (MBO).

MBO is one of those techniques that grew up in the 1970s, surrounded by lots of hype. Management consultancies jumped on its bandwagon, and ran expensive courses to expound its virtues. Whilst it is right to be wary of the objectives(!) of some of these consultancies, there is no doubt that the period did much to bring to the attention of British industry the need for a structured, focused approach. Many company executives reassessed just what their objectives were, and realigned company strategies to suit. It is the ability to clearly focus on objectives in this way that continues to keep many consultants in business – and they continue to be hired by those who have failed to develop it. Have you ever watched Sir John Harvey-Jones – the 'Trouble-shooter' – on TV, sorting out ailing companies? His effectiveness is based largely upon the application of MBO.

Another good example of MBO on TV is the *Challenge Anneka* programme. An extremely tough objective is set, and then everyone becomes intent on seeing the job done; sometimes to the extent of working shifts of 20 hours or more, with little sleep in between. Those taking part share a common objective – and by each member dependably fulfilling their designated tasks and managing resources in such an organized and committed fashion, an amazing amount can be achieved.

11.2.2 Establishing the role of objectives

To appreciate how to manage objectives, it is first necessary to be clear as to what they are exactly. Have you ever realized that objectives rule your life? This morning you got out of bed. You did it because it was your objective to do so. In order to achieve your objective, you carried out a number of tasks, i.e. turned back the covers, swung your legs out, put your feet on the floor and stood up. But what was your objective *exactly*? It was probably that you should get out of bed by a certain *time*. If you continued to stay in bed past the time that you knew you should be up (i.e. lost sight of your objective) you would inadvertently be achieving a different, shorter-term, objective – to remain cosy instead of face the day!

But what made you decide that you needed to get up by a particular time? It was perhaps because your objective was to get to the bus-stop in time, to get to the university, to attend the day's lectures, to gain your degree, to get a good job .... You will note that these objectives are increasingly *long term*. The technique of moving from a shorter-term to a longer-term view of objectives and back again is known as *adjusting the objectives horizon*. As we *raise the horizon* (i.e. take a longer-term view), a fascinating thing happens in that shorter-term objectives become tasks of the longer-term objective. As we *lower the horizon* the last task on that horizon resumes its status as an objective. Careful selection of the last task, i.e. the objective, is vital – as all preceding tasks should be designed to focus upon it.

In the above example, the objective of getting out of bed became a task in achieving the objective of getting to the bus-stop, which in turn became just one task necessary for achieving the objective of attending the day's lectures, and so on.

Some people always seem so organized. You can depend on them to do as they say, be where they need to be. Others struggle to find their way through each day, and soon seem to become overloaded with work. You can probably think of examples of both types – perhaps within your own peer group at university, or amongst your circle of friends – with similar abilities and even similar family commitments, and certainly with the same number of hours in each day! Broadly, they may have the same objectives, but the difference is that the organized ones have intuitively learned to *manage* them. Perhaps you can already identify which type you tend to be – most people are a bit of a mixture. Whatever your natural outlook however, it is important to appreciate that by managing objectives, more can be achieved with the same effort. Or to put it another way, the same can be achieved with *less* effort. Because it is *personal* management, how you apply it is up to you.

11.2.3 Applying the management of objectives

So, you hope to become a systems analyst. This is only one of many careers where you will sooner or later find yourself expected to be a member of a team, responsible for the completion of a sizeable project. Without a clear idea as to what the objectives of the project are, and then a means of managing the project to meet these objectives, the team will flounder and the project will not get completed satisfactorily.

You don't need to wait until you become a systems analyst or other type of team member before discovering the benefits of applying MBO however. For the whole of your life you are going to be ruled by objectives. You cannot help it. You will gain tremendously by being able to identify what these objectives are, and then managing them. How should you go about it?

We will first introduce you to the usefulness of MBO by imagining just one typical scenario that you could encounter as a student. Having done this, we will demonstrate the parallels between your own situation and that of a practising systems analyst.

Let us, then, suppose that you are a student undertaking an essentially practical module in which you have been made a member of a team. The overall objective is to complete a fairly substantial project, lasting a whole semester but broken down into two assignments. Let us further suppose that other teams are in competition with yours, and that there is a special award for the best result for each assignment (you will soon see that this has a significant effect upon the objective). Each student must also take a time constrained test.

There are three major events to be considered:

- assignment 1;
- assignment 2;
- time constrained test.

The successful completion of each event represents the fulfilment of an objective. Each of these will require the completion of a whole series of tasks. But which will be the last one in each case? i.e. which task represents the fulfilment of the objective? And what is the timing for each objective?

You establish that:

- the TCT takes place in semester week 6 – and your last task is to attend it;
- assignment 1 hand-in has a deadline of semester week 7 – and your last task is to submit the last part of it;
- assignment 2 hand-in has a deadline of semester week 14 – and again, your last task is to submit the last part.

In pure MBO terms there are now potentially three *objectives horizons* based upon the timing of these events. If two of the events were targeted to happen at the same time there would be two *objectives horizons* and if all events were planned to occur at once there would be only one.

Objectives horizon 1 – take the time constrained test. What is your objective for the test? How seriously do you take it? Do you simply want to scrape a pass, or would you like to aim for something better?

Objectives horizon 2 – hand in assignment 1. Should it be the team's objective to submit a *good* one? With a bit of thought, and bearing in mind the competitive nature of the course, you may decide that your objective is to prepare the *best* one. Surprisingly, neither of these objectives is really what the course is about – even the second is not specific enough because it does not consider who it is that makes the judgement. Your team's objective should be to produce the *winning* assignment, i.e. the one the *assessor* thinks is the best. You will find that focusing upon an exact objective in this way is a vital part of the process and can have a profound effect upon all sorts of decisions as the project progresses. In this instance it should help you realize the importance of doing exactly what the assignment stipulates, and not wasting time unnecessarily refining areas not mentioned as being important.

If it is assumed that you will need to prepare for the test in some way, the fulfilment of the test and first assignment objectives will require work that is largely to be achieved in parallel. It will be necessary to regularly monitor progress and adjust the attention that each gets at any stage. This is to do with the *scheduling* of the work, and techniques to assist with this are covered in Section 11.4.

Objectives horizon 3 – hand in assignment 2. It is now time to *raise the objectives horizon* and consider assignment 2. Again, it is evident that the objective must be to create the *winning* system.

Simply by careful analysis of what it is you are trying to achieve, you and your team have become *objectives led* – and have identified the ingredient missing from many struggling companies. It is the ability to clearly focus on objectives in this way that keeps many consultancies in business – and gets Sir John Harvey-Jones onto TV!

11.2.4 Tasks and roles

We have already realized that the fulfilment of each objective ends with the successful completion of the last task associated with it. Having identified objectives, therefore, it is necessary to establish tasks, i.e. the work required to achieve each objective, broken down into 'deliverable' stages.

Let us return to the above example. In preparation for the time constrained test, it will undoubtedly be a good idea to attend lectures and tutorials, to ensure you have copies of all handouts, to check that you know the likely content of the paper, and to revise the required subject matter until you are happy that your understanding meets the standard that you have set.

Each lecture, each self-study period etc. can be considered to be a task. In MBO such a task is called *time dependent* – once the time has been spent, the task is complete. If revision of a particular subject area is chosen as being a task – perhaps checking understanding against last year's test – in MBO terms this would be said to be *target dependent*, because completion of the task is dependent upon achieving a certain level of understanding – no matter how long it takes.

To create tasks for the assignments you would follow the same process, the extra complication here being that the whole team is involved. If you read further you will soon appreciate how the team members would be allocated overall functional roles. Tasks would now be matched to members accordingly, possibly with some refinement of roles to compensate for any imbalance of workload. It would be important to keep on referring carefully to the assignment instructions. It may be that each assignment is to be broken down into separate components. Proper use of such information is the key to the allocation of members to roles and tasks – and this is fundamental to the process of changing a group of people into a team.

You didn't realize there was a difference? You will soon, but first let us apply the above scenario to a work-based one. For whilst the above may be very interesting, and may be useful to you while you are a student, what is it doing in a book which purports to turn you into a useful systems analyst?

Well, as explained in the introduction to this chapter, there are many parallels between the module-based scenario described above and the one in which you will be expected to work as a fully-fledged practitioner. Whilst we can assume that you will then have attained a point in your career when the delights of time constrained tests are best forgotten(!), you could have become a member of a software development company given the opportunity to respond to an invitation to tender, in competition with other companies. The client expects a written proposal to be submitted, a demonstration of a prototype, and a short presentation. The written proposal is to be submitted two weeks in advance of the presentation and demo, both of which are to take place on the same day.

As with the student assignments, the overall objective must be clearly established, which is again the need to produce the winning solution, the one the client likes best. It is then necessary to establish the objectives horizons. In this instance the most obvious approach is to select two, i.e. the day on which the written proposal is to be submitted, and the day of the presentation and prototype demo.

Once the MBO approach has been used to identify the tasks needed to complete an objective it is necessary to plan the completion of these tasks, firstly by allocating them to appropriate members of the team. Often, sub-teams are formed: each with the responsibility for establishing and working towards their own objectives within the broader context. Various techniques exist to help with this, one of the most useful being covered in Section 11.4.

MBO is a key to successful personal and team management. Once you get the hang of it, be sure to mention this on your CV. Many companies appreciate its worth and will be impressed that you know how to apply it. Before you can, there are two more concepts that you need to be clear about – how to create a team, and how to manage a project that uses one.

11.3 Establishing who you will be working with

11.3.1 The difference between a group and a team

First we have to get definitions clear – so let's turn to the dictionary ...

'Group – a number of persons or things placed or classified together'
'Team – a group of people working together for a common purpose'

(Collins English Dictionary)

The difference is that the members of a team *work together* to achieve a *common objective*.

11.3.2 How to turn a group into a team

The first stage in creating a team is always to select the group members. Sometimes when groups are formed within courses students are asked to choose who they wish to work with. On other occasions group members are chosen by staff – perhaps by allocating names alphabetically, or selection being engineered on some other basis.

This is certainly what happens in 'real life' – business-based project teams inevitably being created on the basis of providing a wide mix of the necessary skills.

There are essentially three more stages which lead to the successful creation of a team:

- Establish ground rules.
- Identify tasks.
- Based upon identified tasks, allocate roles. These may be largely *organizational* (primarily involved with the team itself, e.g. project leader, minute taker) or *functional* (primarily involved with the completion of the project, e.g. software developer, designer, hardware expert).

If you do all of the above you will be in a good position to *maintain* the team. This involves two essential ingredients: *communication* and *commitment*. Regular meetings and other contact, honest reports about progress, resolving conflicts, doing what you say when you say you will – these are the components which allow a group to work as a team.

Depending upon the size of the project, it is often recommended that the whole team meet together at least once per week, with meetings for sub-teams (e.g. the software developers, system designers etc.) in between as necessary. Full minutes of meetings are not usually necessary, but a record of actions and comments on progress should be maintained for each. This should always record the date/time/venue of the meeting together with an attendance list, and may typically contain details of techniques that have been used, which tasks have been progressed or completed, and which new ones are now to be commenced, with members clearly identified against actions.

Techniques may equip you with the tools to carry out fairly sophisticated systems analysis, to identify and plan objectives, but it is *communication*, *co-operation* and *collaboration* which will enable you to actually do the job.

11.4 Controlling it all

11.4.1 Introducing project scheduling

The planning of time is always an important activity when objectives have to be achieved by a given date – perhaps an anniversary present to buy, or an assignment to be done. It is particularly important when an objective demands that a *group* of people work in a co-ordinated manner. Proper organization makes a tremendous difference to the effort required in meeting such objectives; allowing more time for family and social commitments.

The following instructions describe a simple set of procedures which provide an initial plan, and then a means of continuously monitoring progress – allowing timely adjustments to be made, and therefore preventing last-minute panics. Whilst project management software packages such as *Microsoft Project* and *CA Superproject* are now commonly used to control projects, it is important that you understand the concepts which follow. You will not only gain an appreciation of how such packages work, but will have the advantage that should you ever consider them a bit 'heavy' for a small project you will have the 'paper based' method to fall back on.

The first key point that should be noted is the difference between *elapsed* time (i.e. the time which passes during progress of the project) and *activity* time (i.e. the time actually spent carrying out the work involved).

11.4.2 How to go about it

Establish objectives

Begin by establishing *terms of reference*, i.e. what is *expected* of you. These can be viewed as *external* objectives, or are sometimes called *imposed* objectives. In establishing these, students should take care to note instructions such as:

'in no less than 2000 words, investigate the benefits of ...' (i.e. guidelines being stipulated as to the *size* of the project);

'estimated time for assignment is 40 hours' (i.e. guidelines being stipulated as to the *time to be spent* on the project);

'ensure that due regard is given to questions of reliability and security' (i.e. guidelines being stipulated as to the *content* of the project).

Once these external objectives are established, identify any *internal* ones. These are objectives which are perceived as being necessary or desirable within the project, whilst not having been stipulated as a project requirement. It may be for instance that certain members of a project team would like to use the experience to gain further practice in programming skills, interview the client, or prepare and/or give a presentation. Whilst there will always be jobs which no-one wants and which, therefore, need to be allocated by negotiation, where possible it is often a good idea to give people tasks which they have chosen, because they are then more likely to be committed to them.

Create a task list

All objectives, however determined, are achieved by carrying out certain *tasks*. Sometimes simply the terms of reference will indicate the tasks involved, whereas on other occasions – typically longer and/or group projects – the transition from objectives to tasks will need to be worked out carefully.

However the tasks are derived, the absolute rule is that every task should produce a *deliverable*, i.e. something which can be 'ticked off' as having been achieved. A task called *Continue reading Microsoft Access Manual* is not good enough – but *Read Microsoft Access Manual chapter 2 and complete associated exercises*, is. The deliverable is the exercise answers.

The simplest task list will have the following headings:

Task reference – task description – estimated hours/days – actual hours/days
(e.g. A,B etc.)   (each being e.g. 16/2 for an 8 hr day)

When completing the list note that it is recommended that:

- every objective should involve a minimum of five tasks;
- no task should exceed around 10 hours of work (i.e. activity time)

Keeping to these rules, you should be able to complete tasks often enough to maintain your interest, or (more importantly) take corrective action if necessary.

As each task is entered, firstly show the *activity* time only, as estimated *hours*. Then, decide how many hours per day on average is going to be allocated to achieving the objective, and enter the *elapsed* time accordingly, as a number of *days*.

Create a schedule chart

The schedule chart is the means by which progress is monitored. Several types have been developed, for example:

Gantt charts (so called after their inventor) are perfectly adequate at showing straightforward *sequencing* of tasks. They are easy to prepare and read.

Network charts were designed to address a weakness of Gantt charts, and clearly show *dependencies* of tasks upon one another. They are somewhat complicated to work out however, and difficult to amend.

GASP charts fairly successfully overcome the weaknesses of both of the above, and we will concentrate on these. They retain the clear graphical presentation of the Gantt chart, whilst allowing sequenced, parallel and dependent tasks to be easily portrayed. GASP stands for Graphical procedure for Analytical and Synthetical evaluation and review of construction Programs – or perhaps it is what you do (i.e. gasp) when you are told the full title! Most project management software uses GASP chart principles, although often (wrongly) crediting them as being Gantt-based.

Creating a GASP chart is, fortunately, easier than remembering the words behind the acronym. The one in Figure 11.1 shows a chart as at day 5 of a project. The

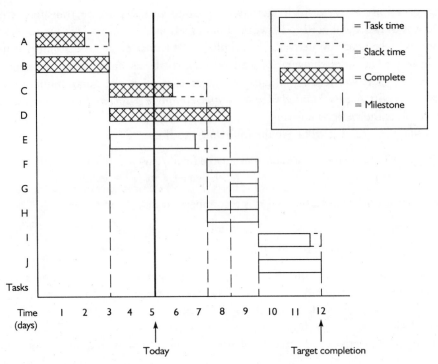

Figure 11.1   A simple GASP chart.

creation of such a chart usually proves to be illuminating in establishing the content of a project, and once complete it provides a vitally effective means of monitoring and control.

According to Figure 11.1:

- tasks A and B are complete;
- task C is ahead of schedule;
- task D is complete, ahead of schedule;
- task E is not started, and is behind schedule;
- tasks F–J are not yet started.

The stages in drawing the chart are as follows. First draw an X (horizontal) axis and Y (vertical) axis – in the same way as for drawing a graph. List the references of all the identified tasks on the Y axis, and mark days (1,2,3 etc.) on the X axis. Then enter a *bar* line for each task with its length appropriate to the elapsed days established at the task list stage – and do not overlook special days (e.g. family occasions etc.) when no activity will be able to take place, adjusting to suit.

An important aspect when considering the starting point for any bar-line, is the need to decide whether the task is dependent upon any others. Using the GASP convention, dotted lines can be used to extend shorter bar lines up to what is called a *milestone* or *key point* denoted by a dotted vertical line. This is a stage at which all preceding tasks have to be complete before a subsequent (i.e. dependent) one can commence, and its position is fixed by the longest preceding bar line. Bar lines which have dotted sections thereby denote the *slack* time in the project. The path through the tasks which incorporates all bar lines *without* dotted sections is the *critical path* for the project. In the example in Figure 11.1, the critical path would be described as B,D,G,J.

When all task bar lines have been drawn, the total estimated days of the project will be indicated. By applying the expected start date, the projected completion date will be calculated. The terms of reference may however include a specified completion date. If so, some adjustment of task activity times, or allocated hours per day, may be necessary. Always assume that the first version of the chart will not be the final one!

Backward and forward scheduling

The process described above uses primarily what is termed *forward scheduling*, i.e. the tasks were entered on to the chart starting with the *first* one, and after all tasks were entered the likely *completion* date was *determined*. If this exceeded a known requirement for completion time, the chart was then adjusted. This procedure is most appropriate however to those occasions when you have been asked to *estimate* a completion time. On other occasions, the completion time is *stipulated*, and you are using the chart to determine how to meet the stipulation. For this it is most appropriate to use *backward scheduling*. This involves listing all of the tasks down the Y axis in the same order as before, but then adding the bar lines beginning/with the *last* task, and ensuring that it ends at the stipulated completion date (or a sensible time beforehand, to allow for problems). If it is discovered that one or more tasks should have begun before today, more time per day will need to be allocated; beginning with those tasks on the *critical path*.

Whichever approach is used, when all adjustments are complete draw a neat version of the chart. This will now be used to monitor progress.

During the project

As soon as the project commences, mark the start date and, therefore, also the expected end date, on the X axis of the GASP chart. Then begin recording progress by thickening the bar lines, indicating the rough proportion of each task which has been completed. In this way, comparison of the thickened lines against the days on the X axis will easily show whether the project is ahead of or behind time. As tasks are completed, enter the *actual* hours and days on the task list (see the section *Create a task list* above). These actual times will prove useful for the future, when planning a similar project.

There is an approximately 90% chance that the project will begin to run behind schedule, a 5% chance that it will run on time, and a 5% chance that it will run early. In 95% of cases therefore, it will be necessary to adjust the schedule during progress of the project. The important thing is to *always work to the latest schedule*, i.e. never be afraid to re-plan and, in particular, never simply assume that it will be possible to catch up on a schedule which is running late.

Scheduling project teams

When controlling a whole team, a schedule chart should be created for each individual member, or if sub-groups are formed within the team, at least for each sub-group. An overall chart should also be created for the whole team, with each task identified with the team member or sub-group name. The team project manager should maintain regular contact with all team members, and keep the charts up to date. This is really where project management software comes into its own.

11.4.3 A simple scheduling exercise

To end this section, you may like to try the following simple exercise which is designed to cover the aspects described above.

Imagine that you have to decorate a room.

1. List the tasks involved, creating a task list in the format shown.

Task ref.	Task description	Estimated		Actual	
		Activity hours	Elapsed days	Activity hours	Elapsed days
A	Decide overall colour scheme	4	1		
B	Work out amount of paint required	1	0.25		
C	Work out amount of wallpaper required				
D					

2. Prepare a GASP chart for these tasks, which should include an indication of at least two dependencies (note for instance that wallpapering cannot commence until the wallpaper has been obtained, and probably only after the painting has been done!).

11.5 CASE tools

11.5.1 From pencils and paper to CASE

Earlier chapters have assumed that all of the systems analysis techniques introduced by us are tackled with a pencil and paper, any cross-checking between diagrams being done by an analyst comparing manually produced diagrams. This is the best way to learn about the techniques, and is also often the way in which these techniques are put into practice on a day-to-day basis. This being the world of computing, however, you could well imagine that a lot of these functions could be computerized.

You would be right, for alongside developments in the way that systems are developed have come automated tools to help the systems analyst control the often complicated procedures and diagrams with which they are faced. These tools come under the broad heading of *CASE* (computer-aided software engineering) *tools* and range from simple diagramming aids to extremely sophisticated computer products that document and automate the whole development life cycle, even generating the final computer code. The term CASE refers to any computer-based facility which attempts to improve the performance of a systems development task, but usually excludes compilers, programming languages and fourth-generation languages. CASE tools can, therefore, include such components as diagramming tools, data dictionaries, report or screen generators, program code generators and project management tools.

Upper CASE tools support the analysis and design stages, providing graphics and text facilities to create and maintain data and structured analysis and design techniques. They help document system requirements, develop and maintain data and process models, or even create simulated interactive user dialogues: this last facility often proving particularly useful for those analysts who aim to produce a first-time user-acceptable system. Some have built-in rules that provide error-checking and cross-referencing, e.g. by editing a data model and highlighting any detected errors.

Lower CASE tools support the design and construction stages of the systems development process. Automatic code generators convert the results of the physical design into code that is suitable for the target hardware and software environment. The code that is generated should be relatively free from syntax errors.

11.5.2 CASE and the systems analyst

The initially most obvious way in which CASE can help the systems analyst is by alleviating the need to draw by hand the graphic representations of an existing system's specification or the design of a new one. Such a view of the advantages of CASE is however a superficial one, for an analyst could use an ordinary graphics package to do this. The principal features which characterise a CASE tool however include:

- the ability to integrate other productivity tools such as project managers, cost–benefit analysis tools and spreadsheets;
- a quality assurance capability which checks for consistency and completeness;
- the ability to share diagrams and data with other systems;
- rapid prototyping.

The functional capabilities of CASE products are built around a *data dictionary* which acts as the central repository for all of the products produced. This repository is really simply a database about an information system project. Not only does it store these products, it also acts as a quality control by making sure that the products are consistent with each other. It performs the functions of storing, organizing, updating analysing, and reporting all data items and objects needed to create, enhance or maintain the information system. So, for example, data flows will be stored in the data dictionary and these data flows will contain data items that are stored in entities within the system. The data dictionary would store a description of this data item once only and link it to the data flows and the entity in which it plays a part. As a system develops and gets more and more complex, it is quite possible for the same thing to appear in more than one guise, and for the analyst to think of them as two different things and give them two different names. A properly controlled and managed data dictionary should help in trapping such inconsistencies and problems.

The data dictionary is the single, authoritative source of every detail about a project. As such, it is a key asset to the project team. It is also invaluable when considering system changes associated with system maintenance.

During the *analysis* stage, the analyst may use an *upper* CASE tool to create and enter many objects into the repository (e.g. user requirements, process models, data models, report layouts, screen formats, data definitions etc.).

During the *design* stage, the analyst may use a *lower* CASE tool to access the data in the repository and automatically generate a first-cut physical design of the system, which is then reviewed and updated as necessary.

Once everything is finalized, a *lower* CASE tool may be used to *generate program code.* Currently something like 25–99% of code can be generated in this way – the remainder having to be modified or added to by hand. *Provided that everything that preceded the code generation was done correctly*, the system should now meet the needs of the users.

The main obstacle to widespread use of CASE tools has been a lack of standards. CASE tools are often incompatible with each other and do not interface properly with other software products. Some products are now emerging, however, which make a serious attempt to integrate with widespread analysis techniques and software. Select Systems is one example of a company with a product which allows a design created using SSADM analysis techniques to be turned into a *Microsoft Access/Visual Basic*-based fully operational system.

11.5.3 Not a substitute for analysis abilities

A systems analyst using a CASE tool is similar to a manager using a word processor. It is still possible to write a poor report using a word processor, although the spelling and grammar should at least be OK. In the same way, it is perfectly possible to use sophisticated CASE tools to create a system which does not fulfil user requirements. We have deliberately not spent a great deal of time discussing CASE tools. This book's title makes it clear that the aim is to ensure you *understand systems analysis techniques* – for if your application of the techniques is flawed, it does not matter how sophisticated the CASE tool is, you will still end up with mistakes. However, we do not wish to underestimate the importance of such tools as they are extremely widespread and very successful. Our advice is not to let the tools take over the development process. It is extremely important that the analyst is in control of the tool and not the other way round. We have witnessed analysts getting so carried away with the sophistication offered by some CASE tools that they have forgotten that the system is being produced for someone other than themselves.

Summary

This chapter began by clarifying the role of the systems analyst. It went on to describe the concept of *Management By Objectives*, how to turn a group of people into a co-ordinated project team, and how to control it all. It has ended with a brief look at computer-aided software engineering.

Further reading

Brown, *Successful Project Management in a Week*, Hodder and Stoughton, London, 1992.

A. K. Johnston, *A Hacker's Guide to Project Management*, Butterworth–Heinemann, Oxford, 1995.

Parkinson, *Making CASE Work*, NCC Blackwell, 1991.

Willcocks and Morris, *Successful Team Building in a Week*, Hodder and Stoughton, London, 1995.

Book summary

This book is, after all, a systems analysis techniques text book – and as such may not *all* have been a rivetting read! We have tried as authors, however, to pass on some of the enthusiasm that we have for the subject, our aim being to make the preceding chapters as interesting and useful as possible. We hope that you have found them so. Whilst the book as a whole concentrates upon systems analysis techniques, the first and last chapters were intended to put these into context, and thus prepare you further for the exciting and demanding world of systems analysis. We recommend the text below as an excellent supplement to this one as it covers in detail the skills which you will need to put the techniques into practice in the *real world*.

We hope that through these pages you have been helped in your understanding of systems analysis – perhaps initially for the purpose of passing an exam, but maybe as a foundation for your future career.

We wish you every success.

Further reading

T. Warner, *Communication Skills for Information Systems*, Pitman, London, 1996.

Index